WILLIAM BLAKE

MASTERS OF MODERN ART

Uniform with this volume

RENOIR.

GAUGUIN.

CÉZANNE.

MONET.

PISSARRO.

BERTHE MORISOT.

MANET.

COROT.

LOUIS BARYE.

VAN GOGH.

RODIN.

CONSTABLE.

FANTIN-LATOUR.

MILLET.

MERYON.

TOULOUSE-LAUTREC.

THE BODLEY HEAD

WILLIAM BLAKE

By PHILIPPE SOUPAULT
Translated by J. LEWIS MAY
With forty illustrations

LONDON

JOHN LANE THE BODLEY HEAD LIMITED

1928

Made and printed in France by
Les Éditions Rieder, 7, place Saint-
Sulpice, Paris.

LIST OF ILLUSTRATIONS[1]

(1) For the photographs of the works reproduced in the present volume the publishers are indebted in all cases to Mr Fred. Hollyer, Pembroke Square, Kensington, W. 8.

WILLIAM BLAKE

E NGLAND, the home of respectability, has witnessed the birth of some strange and occasionally praeterhuman geniuses. None of her sons, howewer, was more utterly disconcerting to her sense of propriety than William Blake, « Mad Blake » as he came, later on, to be called.

Perhaps there never was a man who more thoroughly merited the title of genius than this poet-engraver whose sole ambition was to be himself, and that, to the fullest possible degree. Moreover his genius was so manifest that none who knew him could withhold their tribute of admiration for what their sense of decorum compelled them to call his madness. Blake quickly succeeded in freeing himself from the trammels of time and space, in sundering once for all every bond that might have fettered him to ordinary mundane existence. He dwelt in a supernatural world, where criticism and irony were not, well out of range of the bursts of sardonic laughter which mount up from the spawning earth.

Inevitably, the people with whom he was brought into daily contact, as well as those who gave careful and sympathetic study to his work, floundered more or less fatally in their esti-

mate of him, because they would insist on treating him as a
being of this world. One of his panegyrists, a poet who doubt-
less deserves credit for being the first to recognise the mar-
vellous character of his works, I refer to Algernon Charles
Swinburne, went, as I think, brilliantly astray when he pro-
claimed him to the world as 'a man of mist and fire'. Alike in
his life and in his works we search in vain for anything calculated to support the theory that Blake was a mysterious or fuli-
ginous personage. His career, whatever the legends about him
may suggest to the contrary, was not a tragic one, and the
course of it was as clear and limpid as his own soul.

It is this simplicity which brings Blake before us unmista-
keably as what we call a phenomenon. For the *intelligentsia* of
his times, no less than of our own, an artist had to be com-
pounded, if one may so put it, of a certain admixture of refine-
ment, complexity and eccentricity. He had to be the sort of
being we should have to forgive, no matter to what length his
whims, or even his passions, might lead him. But that a simple
man (I use the word in all its senses) should import his simplicity into his very work — pictures, poems and engravings —
that was altogether too much of a good thing, too much for
ingrained ideas and crystallised preconceptions.

Nevertheless Blake's simplicity is a thing that must be insisted upon, even if the most glowing legends have to go by the
board in consequence. He always refused to adopt a pose. No
matter what the object of his contemplation, whatever he saw,
on the stage, in nature or in everyday life, William Blake refused to gloss it over, to explain it away. His swift reactions, his
spontaneity of thought and feeling, never failed him.

I hardly know whether to admire this constancy of his genius or merely to record its purity. This purity is in fact one
of the most conspicuous of Blake's attributes ; and to avoid
all risk of misunderstanding, it would be as well if we endeavoured to define its character. Blake was an idealist who, of

set purpose, kept aloof from everything, whether near or remote, which, directly or indirectly, could remind him of the
material world. He deliberately held on his solitary way,
never looking back, never making terms with the world. It
was this stern determination, coupled with that love of the
absolute, which was part of his profession of faith, that led
him to that purity which was the guiding principle of his life.
It is no exaggeration to say that he *lived* his purity. It is in the
light of this elemental purity that we must study the life of
Blake and estimate its effect upon his work. It would moreover
be an arbitrary thing to try to consider his life apart from his
work and so to sunder his personality into two distinct sec-
tions. Rarely indeed do we meet in the life of a painter, an
engraver and a poet (Blake was all these things) a unity so
complete. But let there be no mistake, we are not enquiring
whether and to what extent he was a professional or an ama-
teur. No man ever had less of the professional artist about
him than Blake; yet no man was ever more deeply absorbed
than he, in what we may call his earthly remains, that is to say
his works.

All this it is that furnishes the key to a life that winged its
way unfalteringly to the heights. It is this freedom from alloy,
this *oneness* of mind and character, that makes Blake one of
the greatest of men, that is to say a man who makes us feel
most sure that there is an element of greatness in humanity.

PART I

WILLIAM Blake was born on the 20th November
1757. The origin of his family is obscure; but we
know that his father had Irish blood in his veins.
William was the second of a family of five children and he was a long way from being spoilt at home. His

father kept a hosier's shop in Broad Street, Golden Square, which was then on the outskirts of London. As he manifested a taste for drawing, his parents sent him to an art school where he assisted the master and learnt elementary drawing. He was a dreamy and imaginative child. « I came into the world » he said of himself, « like a spirit hidden in a cloud ». Perpetually filled with wonder at the discoveries he made, he loved to talk at large about them. When he was eight years old he began to have visions, or rather to tell his parents about them, for he confessed that when he was no more than four, he had seen the Eternal, face to face. God leaned his hoary visage against the window-pane and the little boy burst into tears. Sometime afterwards he saw a tree laden with angels. On another occasion he told his mother he had seen Ezekiel sitting under a tree. His parents jeered at his fibs as they called them and smacked him to teach him to speak the truth. Blake however went on telling his artless stories in utter good faith. He was not in the least scared at these visions, which seemed to him the most natural things in the world; nor was he perturbed at these extraordinary encounters, for his relations with God and Ezekiel were perfectly friendly and familiar with nothing in them calculated to alarm or overwhelm. Of course people laughed at him, and his drawing master would tell him to « be quiet ».

He loved to wander about the London streets admiring the drawings and engravings in the shop windows. And it often happened that as he stood gazing in for a long time, they invited him to go inside, and he became a sort of habitué. He came to be known as 'the little connoisseur' for he was always quite ready to give his opinion and to discourse at length. He was just as innocent as ever and some of the things he said would cause his hearers much amusement.

Blake's childhood affords a key to the whole of his subsequent existence. The child was father to the man. His character never changed, he never « mended his ways ». The parental chastisements, the jeers of his classmates, made no impression upon him. He just went on seeing his visions and telling about them with customary *naïveté* and childish grace.

Blake's disposition never suffered, despite the gibes he had to put up with. All through life he felt a crying need to unburden his soul. This need which grew daily more insistent rather chafed at the engraver's « craft » into which he was being initiated with the hundred and one little pettifogging difficulties which his teachers conjured up to his imagination.

When he was about eleven years old, he felt a craving for self-expression and not feeling quite at home enough in the art to engrave what he wanted to say, he put it into poetry.

He was now put with Pars a draughtsman with an establishment in the Strand, where he worked with assiduity. He held himself aloof from his family, realising now that he did not belong to their race, and he set out to discover a world of his own. Bending over his Bible he was filled with wonder as he heard the prophets cry aloud and wept as he thought on the sufferings of Job. All these exalted beings had by this time become more intimate, more closely akin to him than his own folk and the mocking crowd about him. It was during this period that Blake, quite as a matter of course, slipped away from the material world to explore those realms of mystery which he gradually made his own and to which he never more bade adieu. Whilst he was being taught to make copies of old models, his thoughts took flight and winged their way to the heights where the spirits of the great discourse and sit in meditation. With them he was henceforth to take up his abode, drawing ever nearer and nearer to them, so near that they became his friends, his only friends, and so close to him that it did not amaze him to encounter them in the streets of London.

Sometimes his father would take umbrage at Blake's complete absorption in his trade and his submissive attitude to-

wards the poor little tasks he was called on to perform. Before
long he came to the conclusion that it was time for William to
have a new master and he decided to pick out a well-known
man for the purpose, an influential man, a man to push him
on in the world. He therefore took the young man to see Ry-
land the painter, who stood high in the royal favour and was a
friend of the Court poets. As soon as he set eyes on him Blake
grew suddenly pale and tried to get away. He stoutly refused
to be taught by him and when urged to tell the reason he shou-
ted excitedly « He will be hanged, he will be hanged... ». His
father, overwhelmed with confusion, dragged the boy away
and rated him soundly. Twelve years later the painter received
short and sharp shrift at the hangman's hands. He was executed on a charge of embezzling the funds of the East India Company.

So, another teacher had to be sought and finally William
was sent to Bazire, an engraver who merits attention because
he exerted a real and pernicious influence on his pupil, curbing
and corrupting his originality.

Bazire had lived long in Rome and was a fervent admirer of
Michael-Angelo. When he returned to London, with a perfect
mastery of his craft, he won much admiration and secured a
good appointment. His monotonous, arid and rather common-
place style coupled with his undeniable ability brought him in
a large amount of lucrative and fashionable business. He became engraver-in-ordinary to Hogarth and Reynolds.

Whatever we say about him, however, we must admit that
he realised the stuff his pupil was made of and backed him up
through thick and thin.

William stuck to his work and whipped himself into following his master's principles. But he was not backward, while
working, in telling his fellow pupils all about his meetings
with Prophets and his talks with the various heroes of the
Bible. As may well be imagined, they roared with laughter at

him, and he began to be known among them as « Mad Blake ».

The youthful William was too much of a man to put up with gibes that often enough struck home. He did nor hesitate to give as good as he got. Hardly a day went by without a set-to. Bazire, who had the youngster's interests at heart, saw that he would have to be kept apart. So he sent him to Westminster Abbey and made him do the rounds of the old churches in London copying sculptures and making extracts from documents. Blake took wholeheartedly to the job and fell violently in love with Gothic, which is worth noting, in view of the disrepute into which the Middle Ages and all their works had fallen at the time. It was a passion that sundered him irrevocably from the technical superficialities then so much in vogue. He could not bear being thwarted and longed hungrily for solitude. One day, when he was at work in the Abbey perched up on some scaffolding, a schoolboy climbed up to where he was and began to interrupt him. Blake flew into a passion, and with one blow of his fist, knocked the intruder headlong.

These youthful days were full of profit for Blake. He found out what he was, or more correctly what he was not and never would be ; that is to say a child of the age. Setting at nought his master's precepts, his father's prayers and his comrades' example, Blake refused point blank to have anything to do with « the fashion ». He buried himself deep in a complete isolation of spirit. He flung himself with passionate eagerness into the study of mediaeval art, striving to interpret the significance of its symbolism. While his spirit drew ever farther and farther away from the common daily round, growing careless of the world about him, he abandoned himself to the flood that bore him ever nearer and nearer to the Middle Ages. Strange scenes beheld by him only served to strengthen this attitude of mind or shall we say this psychic state. One day he was present at the exhumation of Edward the First whose body appeared in a perfect state of preservation, clothed in a sumptuous robe, with the crown upon his head and the sceptre in his hand.

Despite this attitude, despite these portentous happenings, he went on working steadily, spurred on by poverty. However thankless the task, he remained undaunted, and returning home after the day's work was over, he would settle down to do some engraving on his own account and continue his labours far into the night. He was fond of his craft and at a time when painting in oils was so much in favour, this predilection on his part for the means of direct expression is singular to say the least of it. Moreover he looked to the Middle Ages for *motifs* to justify his preference for engraving over the prevailing taste for painting in oils. He was sixteen when he completed his first original engraving (1773), *Joseph of Arimathea among the Rocks of Albion*. Some explanatory lines upon it run thus :

« This is one of the Gothic artists who built the Cathedrals in those days which we call the dark ages, wandering, clad in the skins of goats and sheep, and of whom the world was unworthy. Such were the Christians of every Age. »

When he was thirteen Blake found himself involuntarily, intuitively shall we say, in revolt against the spirit of his age. And so that the reaction should be the more thorough, his instinct led him towards the eternal. While he was yet a youth, the young engraver set out to seek the things that are great, things to lift him above the niceties and affectations dear to the eighteenth century. From his very earliest days he revealed himself a fighter, one who had made up his mind to fight, not because he loved fighting for its own sake, or because he delighted in the excitement of the combat, but simply because he could do no other, because he could not put his soul in bondage. While he was yet little more than a child, he was, even then, in all essentials, the man who was one day to declare

« I should grieve to possess earthly glory, for everything that a man wins in the way of material glory detracts from his spiritual glory. I want nothing. I am quite happy. »

As a rest from his engraving work, he wrote poetry and read eagerly. But his choice of reading matter was as strange as, if we bear in mind the tastes of the time, it was significant. He liked the poems of Chatterton and he had a passion for Ossian. Blake's profound and precocious love of poetry was a most important factor in the formation of his character. It is a taste that, in the first place, marks him off from the generality of engravers, who were far too deeply concerned with the technicalities of their art, and secondly it helped him to subordinate art to intellect, and continually to renew the sources of his inspiration. Blake, in fact, was not merely a writer of poetry ; poetry was the very breath of life to him and shed an aureole about everything he wrought. It was, in a word, the mainspring of every significant thing that he achieved. It was his poetry, moreover, that furnished a text to those critics who found fault with his work because in their opinion it was too *literary*.

On reaching his twenty-first year, he severed his connection with Basire and went to work at the Royal Academy, on the advice of Moser, a Swiss, the new royal favourite and the friend of Reynolds. This new teacher was anxious that Blake should copy Rubens and the French school. But as usual he rejected this advice and, deaf alike to entreaties and commands, he had recourse to earlier models. First he devoted himself to Raphael and next to Michael-Angelo. What people used to call his spirit of contradiction, made him admire a painter of battle scenes and great historic events. Mortimer was his name, and his day was long since over. Like Mortimer he tried to *compose* and thus made himself a target for not a few sarcastic criticisms.

What strikes us as remarkable is that one can discern in the youthful Blake the broad outlines of his after career and trace the main currents of his genius. Just as if he foresaw what he was afterwards destined to become, he occupied himself energetically and exclusively with whatever things were germane to the formation of his individuality. He never hesitated. He made up his mind at once. Almost straightway he would seize upon whatever was congruous with the substance and character of his work. He acted as if he could see into the future. When we come to study Blake and his work it seems beside the mark to speak of influence. An influence is not so much a swift lightning flash of illumination, as a gradual process of enchantment. But Blake yielded himself body and soul to the call of the future. Now and henceforth he had no interests save poetry and the engraver's art. He was still living at his father's, hidden away in the little hosier's shop in Broad Street careless of his surroundings, which in fact, had not altered since his childhood. He worked for anyone who was willing to give him a job, living on very little and seemingly quite contented with his poverty, since neither his dreams nor his work were affected thereby.

But now, behold, a new influence came into his life. That new influence, Flaxman, was the first to realise the full extent of his genius. He took it upon himself to give him counsel, to extend a helping hand. Flaxman was a sculptor, somewhat of a « climber » perhaps, but certainly not lacking either in taste or ability. Acquaintance soon ripened into friendship. The two companions took up their quarters and lived together. Hitherto Blake's interests had been almost entirely monopolised by engraving, save for an occasional interruption in favour of poetry. But now he became conscious of a new type of emotion that made his heart beat high. Taking a leaf out of his friend's book he began to look with interest upon women. On one occasion he met a little dark haired workgirl in the street and spoke to her. Seeing how shy and bashful he was, the girl began to quiz him for his timidity and thought to indulge in a little coquetry. This annoyed Blake and he went his way without giving her another look. Before long he met another girl and *recognised* her. Going up to her he straightway exclaimed « I love you ». « And I love you » answered the girl simply. Then the flame was kindled in the poet's heart, and in a little while he made her his wife. The young woman, Catherine Boucher, who was henceforth to share his fortunes, was of the humblest origin. She could neither write nor read. According to all accounts she was an extremely engaging young person. Tall and dark with a beautiful complexion, she had a charming smile. She had an even temper, a steadfast nature, an alert and understanding intelligence and she never thought of herself where others were in question.

And so he married her. Catherine, being unable to write, affixed her mark to the marriage register. Blake, still as much in love as ever, set to work to teach her to read and write and, not content with that, to paint and engrave. They took long walks together in the outskirts of London and, as they went their way, Blake would talk and talk, opening his heart to her, exultant, and filled with joy and wonder because someone whom he loved was listening to him with admiration, and because he could at last unburden his soul without the fear of exciting ridicule.

His father, in high displeasure at this humble match, his father who (with a business man's eye to the main chance) had been hoping his son would become something of a lion in the social world, banished the young couple from his establishment. They sought refuge in the artists' quarters, and at length lighted upon a little house close to where Hogarth and Reynolds had lived.

Friend Flaxman and his young wife used to come see them, and they marvelled to behold how simply Blake lived and how hard he worked. Flaxman told his friends all about it, for he

was always something of a lion-hunter, and the friends were
eager to come and inspect the youthful phenomenon. Blake and
his wife were dragged off to be presented to Mrs Matthew whose
salon was frequented by the leading lights of the time. This
Mrs Matthew, who used to read Homer in the original, played
the part of a friend and counsellor to the rising artists and
liked to gather round her all the good-looking women of her
day.

Blake was welcomed with opened arms and introduced to
the company as a new sensation. They made him stand up and
sing his songs. All this soon began to jar on him and he jib-
bed. Back in the shelter of his own home he sat himself down
to write a satirical work to be called *The Island in the Moon*
in whose strange inhabitants the *habitués* of Mrs Matthew's
salon were plainly recognisable. However, his peace of mind
gradually coming back to him, his interest in this book died
out.

Having got through this experience of the world of wit and
fashion, Blake turned his mind to work and poetry. Worldly
fame and worldly riches had no attraction for him. In the
seclusion of his own abode, living in great poverty, his life was
nevertheless a happy one. He devoted himself to the education
of his wife, engraving and writing night and day.

Young as he was, the main trend of his life was already determined. He haunted a world of his own creation, fashioning
it little by little to his own ideas. Everyday he travelled a
little farther from this world of ours, faring on his way towards the infinite. Whenever he paused to look back, the rebel
in him got the upper hand, he must needs hurl defiance and
shock the world.

In 1788 he lost his brother Robert, who was apprenticed to
an engraver. William was grieved at this « departure », as he
put it. But his brother's ghost came back to see him and to
give him aid. It was, declared Blake, his brother's spirit that

taught him a new method of engraving. Then came 1789 and
the French Revolution. William's enthusiasm was at white
heat. He paraded the streets of London with a cap of liberty
on his head, and frequented all the most revolutionary haunts
in the town. He sallied forth to seek out Thomas Paine to
tell him he was going to be arrested, and Paine managed to get
clear away. The Blakes now went to live in Lambeth and there
it was that he was destined to meet, in the person of Thomas
Butt, the man who was to be his protector, who was to lighten
for him the hardships of daily life and rescue him from destitution. Thomas Butt was deeply impressed by the genius of the
youthful Blake, displayed that sedulous respect which is so
typical of the British Maecenas, and eagerly bought up everything the artist put before him. Blake was now able to do as he
liked and was freed, or practically so, from the necessity of
going round seeking for jobs and commissions. Owing to the be-
nefactions of the generous Butt, Blake found leisure to experiment with new engraving processes. Then all of a sudden he
gave up engraving and flung himself into a course of reading.
From now onwards he fell more and more under the spell of the
so-called mystical writers and on the mind and soul of Blake
these writers were destined to exert a decisive influence. With
their aid he was to build up the world in which he was to dwell
henceforth, the world within whose confines he was to conduct his wife, than whom no one was better fitted to share its
marvels. But he never gave up reading the Bible, which for
him was an inexhaustible source of inspiration, and in which
he never sought in vain for friends. Another book that won
his heart completely was Milton's *Paradise Lost*. Blake however did not read it like an ordinary mortal. The influences
under whose spell he came were not mere intellectual adven-
tures. Such wholeheartedness, such feverish intensity did he
bring to his reading that he said farewell for ever to this
sublunary sphere.

At this point we may perhaps quote a few of the stories which never fail to crop up when the name of Blake is mentioned. The reader must beware against looking on the poet-engraver as a madman, or as one subject to hallucinations. That facile way of dismissing him must be guarded against at all costs.

« Who was that you said 'good-day' to? » a friend once asked him when they were out for a walk together.

« That? Why that was the Apostle Paul », replied Blake.

He used to say Swedenborg was the greatest of men, and he used to see Milton, who would come up and speak to him.

« Yesterday I saw Milton », he would observe. « He spoke to me and, in my turn, I tried to tell him he was wrong, but it was no use. »

And when any trouble came upon him and when he had to put forth a special effort, it was to his friends that he appealed for help. He invoked *his friend* Milton, *his friend* King Solomon, who comes and sits for him and who promises when he goes away to come again because the engraver had not been able to work in all the details of his complicated headgear.

Flaxman now introduced Blake to Hayley who was greatly interested in his work and gave him some orders. Then he offered him a cottage at Felpham. Blake entranced by the silent serenity of the country, settled down there and declared the place was like heaven. And he attacked his work with renewed ardour, looking for advice and help to his friends Milton and the Apostle Paul.

It was at Felpham that an incident occurred which made a great impression on Blake. He was strolling one day in the garden when, hearing him talking to himself, a soldier came up and began to laugh and jeer at him. Being thus rudely interrupted in his meditations Blake rushed at the man and kicked him out of the place. Schofield, such was the soldier's name, was determined to be even with him and accused him of

having insulted the army and the King, and of having uttered
all manner of seditious doctrine. Being brought before the ma-
gistrates, Blake had no difficulty in proving his innocence and
the baselessness of the accusations. But he became more terri-
fied of the outer world, more apprehensive of the police than
ever and Schofield, in his eyes, became a sort of personification
of the brute-beast. An allusion to the affair is contained in
the Prophetic Books.

His protector, amazed at Blake's eccentric methods, tried
to get him to modify them ; but the engraver knew very well
who had bidden him work in this manner, and refused to
change his procedure. Hayley insisted and Blake prefered to
say good-bye to « heaven » rather than compromise his liberty
of action. Nevertheless he had dreamed he would be happy
in this region. At the beginning of his stay he wrote to his
friend Flaxman saying : « Felpham is a sweet place for study,
because it is more spiritual than London. Heaven opens here
on all sides her golden gates : her windows are not obstructed
by vapours ; voices of celestial inhabitants are more distinctly heard, and their forms more distinctly seen ; and my
cottage is also a shadow of their houses. ... And now begins a
new life, because another covering of earth is shaken off. I am
more famed in Heaven for my works than I could well conceive. In my brain are studies and chambers filled with books
and pictures of old, which I wrote and painted in ages of eternity before my mortal life ; and those works are the study and
delight of archangels. »

Disillusioned, his faith in friends and friendship shattered,
he went back to London and took up his quarters at n⁰ 17,
South Molton Street. His sole thought now was of his work and
he turned his gaze deliberately inwards. He set to work to
illustrate two poems of his own, *Milton* and *Jerusalem*, which
he had written at Felpham.

And now he who had looked with eagerness and hope to-

wards the dawn of a new life, was henceforth destined to find
his path beset with treachery and disappointment. The period
which extends from his return to London until his meeting
with Linnel is the saddest and most miserable portion of his
whole existence. First of all there was the Cromek affair. Cromek commissioned him to design illustrations for Blair's
Grave and, having promised faithfully that he (Blake) should
engrave them, gave the work to an Italian. This was bad
enough, but another piece of treachery flung Blake into the
deepest despair. This same Cromek, getting to hear that Blake
was busy on a large picture dealing with the Canterbury Tales,
placed an order with Stothard for a picture illustrating the
same subject.

And now we see Blake completely deserted. Friends he has
none, and even those on whom he used to think he could always rely, his heavenly friends, come to visit him no more. He
is overtaken by the direst want. His courage and his faith alike
give way. He arranges to put his big picture *The Canterbury
Pilgrims* on show in Broad Street. It was but a sort of melan-
choly relic, surrounded by other paintings, watercolours and
engravings. However he hoped that this publicity, which, if
the truth must be told, was not altogether to his taste, would
serve to banish misunderstanding, unmask false friends and,
in a word, once more give him a clear field. He drew up a *Descriptive Catalogue* in which he discusses his works, condes-
cends so far as to explain his pictures and intentions and as to
denounce the slanders of his adversaries. In this way he hoped
to win, not indeed earthly glory, which he despised, but at all
events a few orders which would help him to live, as well as
some measure of respect for his work. He entertained great
expectations from this exhibition because he knew that nothing like it had ever before been seen in London, that is to
say nothing like what he himself had beheld with the help of
those glorious friends who had come from the Bible, who had

come back from the realms of Death itself, to lend him aid.
The visitors, few in number, who came to look at his canvases
either burst out laughing or shrugged their shoulders, « What
a madman ! » they would murmur as they took their departure.
Such critics as deigned to notice him at all, openly ridiculed
him. Leigh Hunt in the *Examiner*, displayed particular fero-
city. He ridiculed the painter, belittled the engraver and said
the man himself was mad, not responsible for his actions. Rival
artists who realised that Blake's entire work was a severe con-
demnation of their own, made no attempt to hide their joy at
his discomfiture.

Blake's trials increased. These were days of faint-hearted-
ness, discouragement and despair. He tried to continue the
struggle, but he could not. Neither his poverty nor his faith
availed to conciliate his adversaries. They continued to mock
and jeer, doing their utmost to emphasize his insanity. For
eight years he continued the fight with all his strength. His
poverty increased, his friends deserted him, still he held on.
But in vain. Then at last he abandoned the struggle and for a
time ceased to engrave or to paint.

Of this period of his life we know next to nothing. There are
no references to him in the memoirs of his contemporaries, and
it is probable that, at this time, Blake was seeing no one at all.
He published nothing, contenting himself with jotting down
a note every now and again. But he did no painting, no engraving. Until the year 1817 we have no tidings of him. He was
living in London but, as it seemed, definitely silent, definitely
under a cloud. His defeat seemed to be complete and final.
Only his wife, Catherine Boucher, clung loyally to him.
Blake's life, Blake's attitude had scandalised Society, and Society was taking its revenge.

Perhaps he was dying of hunger. No matter. No one cared.
The story runs that one of the causes of the estrangement of
all respectable people was that one day a man whom he scar-

cely knew came to call on Blake and found him sitting on the floor naked reading Paradise Lost with his wife, also naked.

« Come along in », said Blake to the startled visitor, « we are only Adam and Eve » The story went the rounds, caused much laughter in the regular artistic circles and estranged those few people who still retained some regard for him. The shadows quickly gathered about him and soon his name ceased to be mentioned. No publisher ever sent him an order.

Blake lived under the same roof with Catherine Boucher, his wife, but his companions were Milton, Saint Paul and Ezekiel. The years went by. Occasionally, in connexion with some picture or other, the name of Blake would be mentioned. « What's become of him? » someone would ask. No one knew. Blake never came out of his house. For two years he never left his room. Everyone thought he was dead. He was old, forgotten, in another world.

One day, a day just like any other, Linnel, the famous painter happened to cast his eyes on one of Blake's engravings. He was thunderstruck. Then a smile came over his face. He looked at it again. The desire to laugh had gone. He had a vague recollection of having heard mention of Blake's name. He was the man people said was mad.

« Blake? What's happened to Blake? »

« He is dead, so they say. »

Linnel made enquiries and after a long search discovered him in a little street off the Strand. He was shown an old, silent man who refused to go out of doors.

Linnel told him how greatly he admired him, and purchased a few books and engravings.

He came again and brought his friends Tatham and Mr and Mrs Aders who laid siege to Blake. Gradually a « legend » began to take shape. He was no madman, but a genius. The army of tuft-hunters decided that they must get to know this strange old man, among them Crabb Robinson who kept a diary in

which he narrates the story of his visits to the engraver. Varley
the landscape painter, who was an enthusiastic astrologer, also
came to pay his respects to Blake. It was something like glory,
but it did not affect him at all. He welcomed the people who
came to see him, and who asked questions and bought his drawings — welcomed them with friendly courtesy but without
servility. People still laughed at him and they could not decide
whether to look on him as a madman or as just a harmless old
simpleton. But they were in doubt about his genius. We are
indebted to Henry Crabb Robinson, lawyer, dilettante and
lion-hunter, a man who loved to be in the swim to be up in
the latest sensation, for some memories of Blake set down by
him in his diary which, though private, was certainly intended
to be read. He records certain sayings of Blake that date from
about this period and which throw a light on his intellectual
and moral attitude :

« I will put down as they occur to me without method all
I can recollect of the conversation of this remarkable man.
Shall I call him artist or genius — or mystic — or madman?
Probably he is all. He is now old, pale — with a Socratic countenance and an expression of great sweetness, but bordering on
weakness, except when his features are animated by expression and then he has an air of inspiration about him. The conversation was on art, and on poetry, and on religion ; but it
was my object, and I was successful, in drawing him out and
in so getting from him an avowal of his peculiar sentiments. I
was aware before of the nature of his impressions, or I should
at times have been at a loss to understand him. He was shewn
soon after he entered the room some compositions of Mrs Aders
which he cordially praised. And he brought with him an engraving of his Canterbury Pilgrims for Aders. One of the
figures resembled one in one of Ader's pictures. 'They say I
stole it from this picture, but I did it 20 years before I knew
of the picture. However, in my youth I was always studying

this kind of paintings. No wonder there is a resemblance'. In this he seemed to explain *humanly* what he had done, but he, at another time, spoke of his paintings as being what he had seen in his visions. And when he said 'my visions' it was in the ordinary unemphatic tone in which we speak of trivial matters that every one understands and cares nothing about. In the same tone he said repeatedly, the 'Spirit told me'. I took occasion to say — You use the same word as Socrates used. What resemblance do you suppose is there between your spirit and the spirit of Socrates? 'The same as between our countenances'. He paused and added : 'I was Socrates'. And then, as if correcting himself, 'A sort of brother. I must have had conversations with him. So I had with Jesus Christ. I have an obscure recollection of having been with both of them'.

« ... As connected with this idea, I will mention here (though it formed part of our talk walking homeward) that on my asking in what light he viewed the great question concerning the Divinity of Jesus Christ, he said 'He is the only God' But then he added — 'And so am I and so are you'. Now he had just before been speaking of the errors of Jesus Christ — 'He was wrong in suffering Himself to be crucified He should not have attacked the government. He had no business with such matters'. On my enquiring how he reconciled this with the sanctity and divine qualities of Jesus, he said 'He was not then become the Father'.

« It is easier to repeat the personal remarks of Blake than these metaphysical speculations... He spoke with seeming complacency of himself — said he acted by command. The spirit said to him 'Blake be an artist, and nothing else'. In this there is felicity. His eye glistened while he spoke of the joy of devoting himself solely to divine art. 'Art is inspiration. When Michael Angelo or Raphael, or Mr Flaxman does any of his fine things, he does them in the spirit' ! Blake said 'I should be sorry if I had any earthly fame for whatever natural glory a man has is so much detracted from his spiritual glory... I want nothing whatever. I am quite happy.' »

In spite of the glaring inaccuracies of this report, it is likely enough that, in his intercourse with these new friends, Blake did present an attitude of candid innocence that amazed and perhaps even came as rather a shock to people who expected to discover a phenomenon with a certain admixture of the charlatan.

Thanks to Linnel, Blake was rescued from obscurity and destitution. He received orders, always through Linnel, who encouraged him and backed him up, and he had got back to work again. At the request of Varley, who loved to talk to him about his visions, he made portraits of all his visitors « from on high ». Then he set to work on a large fresco depicting *The Last Judgment* and busied himself with a set of illustrations to *the Book of Job* which Butts had commissioned him to prepare.

In 1828, Blake being then sixty-five, the Royal Academy of London made him a grant of twenty-five pounds.

He did a great deal of painting and engraving during this closing period of his life, but he wrote no more. He seemed now to be living his poetry. The afflatus finds no external manifestation. Henceforth he never did any engraving work unless it was definitely commissioned, and he made no new discoveries in his art. His health had already begun to decline. He felt that he was an old man and that his race was run, yet within him, deep down in his heart, the spirit of youth lived on unconquered. He began to lean even more heavily upon one in whom he had trusted all his life long, upon his wife, who supported him and renewed his fainting courage. He hardly ever got up, and it was on his bed that he did his sketches for an illustrated edition of the *Divina Commedia* (1). It was not

---

(1) Disgusted with the weakness and poverty of the translation he learnt Italian when he was fifty-seven in order to read Dante in the original.

until the end was close at hand that he drew the portrait of his wife. He could no longer rise from his bed because of his swollen ankles and the trouble on his chest.

One of his admirers, T. J. Smith, who was present at his death, records that on the 12th August 1827 he improvised and sang some songs to his Creator which fell sweetly upon the ear of his wife who was in the room. Gazing at her affectionately he said to her, « My beloved those songs are not mine, not mine ! » And then he told her that nothing could separate them and that he would always be beside her to protect her.

It is also said that just before his death, and quite calmly, Blake held converse with his friends « He said he was about to go into that country which all his life long he had desired to explore. »

His end was paceful and he was buried beside his father and mother and beside his brother Robert whom he had loved so well, in the Cemetery of Bunhill Fields.

PART II

I T is not easy to separate the life of Blake from his work, and it is in the light of his life that we must study his work, work so obscure and so puzzling, so childlike yet so full of genius, so admirable in its audacity and in its form and yet so baffling in its weakness. It behoves us also to hear in mind that William Blake was an admirable poet and that he rated poetry very high.

It will not here be my aim to consider which of the two was the greater, the poet or the artist. I will merely remark that we must never lose sight of the poet in our study of the engraver. Another thing which it is important to bear in mind is that Blake's real work in life was engraving, and that poetry was, so to speak, merely a *parergon*.

Blake began to study drawing at a very early age, because he loved the beautiful prints displayed in the London shops, and he begged his father to let him become an artist. If we adopted the customary expression we should say that little William Blake had the artistic vocation. He was a born draughtsman, so much was evident from the ease with which he was able to reproduce, in form and line, the engravings and pictures he set out to copy. Still more convincingly is this brought home to us when we contemplate the compositions which are wholly and solely the fruit of his imagination acting upon things visible to him but which the rest of the world saw not.

We all know what untoward effects the imagination has had on certain painters and into what evil paths it has led them because with them, the thinker was dominated by the craftsman. Looked at in this way the benefits or drawbacks of the imagination are a criterion of any given artist's calibre.

Blake's imagination always served him the more in proportion as it dispensed with models, so that, at the last, he came to rely entirely on his imagination. We shall have again to emphasise the exceptional nature of Blake's imaginative gifts, but here and now, we may see that they conferred upon their owner all the endowments which the art of the draughtsman and engraver demand.

Blake's work may be divided into four parts, each of which is very markedly distinguished from the rest.

The first period extends roughly from 1771 to 1780. These are the years of apprenticeship, the years devoted to the practical acquistion of the engraver's craft. The year 1780 saw the beginning of the second period which extends to about 1788. It was during these years that Blake was acted upon by external influences and at length found himself.

The years from 1788 to 1811 are years of combat, painful but productive years. Blake in full possession of his art, confi-

dent of himself, produces work which, however original, gives
evidence of agitation and feverishness of mind in the artist.

The exhausting struggles and the defeats which set their
seal upon these years, silence the poet's lips and make nerve-
less the engraver's hands ; they are years of obscurity and iner-
tia. It was not until 1817 that Blake returned to his labours
and from then onwards until his death he produced his most
famous work, the work by which he was resolved to stand or
fall.

I. *Apprenticeship Days* (1771-1780)

We know nothing, or nearly nothing, of William Blake's
early efforts. Little is to be gleaned from what his teachers
and his contemporaries had to say about him. According to all
accounts he was an apt pupil and he carried out with assiduity,
the precepts of his teacher. His progress must have been rapid,
since, as early as 1773, Basire sent him to copy the tombs in
Westminster Abbey.

Even then we behold him in revolt against the prevailing
tastes of the day. He began on his *Joseph of Arimathea amid
the rocks of Albion,* a work of obvious distinction.

It is clear that at the end of his apprenticeship he must have
possessed a complete mastery of his art, because he was given
numerous commissions from publishers and booksellers.

II. *External influences* (1780-1788)

No sooner was he free from scholastic bondage, no sooner
was he in full possession of his liberty, than Blake encountered
two men, Stothard and Flaxman, who did their best to bring
their influence to bear upon him. But it was his mode of life
that they sought in influence rather than his art, which had
not yet come to the fullness of its individuality. It was moreover at this period that great changes were in fact introduced

into Blake's life. He married Catherine Boucher, who worshipped him. And now, surrounded by his friends, encouraged by his wife, Blake felt himself free to give full play to his fancy, free to assert his individuality.

The few authentic works which date from this period are for the most part illustrations, in which Blake sacrifices all, or nearly all, to the subject. He takes great pains over the details, but seems to attach small importance to the whole. The various parts, considered in themselves, are remarquable enough and, in each part, the constituent details, the faces for example, are of great artistic value. The background would appear to be a piece of decorative work designed to show up the figures.

In these latter works, dated 1789 (the date may be arbitrary and they were quite possibly earlier work) we can already trace the gifts that were to make Blake famous as an engraver. We see power allied with charm, we discern an almost brutal strength of line mingled with a softness of tone and tint.

Blake is ever seeking, seeking to find himself. Instead of feeling his way as almost all engravers, do, he progresses by leaps and bounds. All the works of this period are different one from another, the obviously lyrical quality in their composition being the only characteristic they have in common. For at this stage of his career, Blake is, so to speak, wholly devoted to poetry. It is to be noted that he is conscious of the lyrical power within him and far from being scared by it, or endeavouring to keep it under control, he encourages it to surge forth with all its energy. And when we consider his life, we see that he never sought to bring it into bondage. He loved Catherine, his wife, with passionate and invincible adoration, and when he gave his friendship he gave it unstintingly, blindly, glorying in the fire that devoured his whole being. Such ardour, such passion could not fail to affect his art and his craftsmanship. Laurence Binyon rightly remarks that since

3

the time of Albrecht Durer the engraver's art had consisted solely in reproducing the works of painters or draughtsmen. It was just about now that Blake deliberately made up his mind to emancipate himself from professional routine and to give up copying drawings and the endeavour to represent colours by lines and chips. Inspired with this determination he made an engraving an original work of art, and no longer a mere adaptation as it had been hitherto.

The *Happy Day* engraved in 1780 but conceived prior to that date, furnishes an example of this emancipation. All the old processes were abandoned in favour of direct expression and the use of purely and specifically technical means of the engraver's art.

It was henceforth Blake's business to perfect this technique and to enlarge its boundaries, and in this endeavour he persisted until the end of his life. For from this time onward Blake set his heart on being an engraver first and foremost. Painting and drawing were but arts ancillary to that aim.

This date in Blake's career possesses an historical importance which we must in no wise overlook. Those painters and artists who rediscovered Blake at the end of his life, and those who, after his death, hailed him as a master, were not deceived, and it was on Blake the engraver that they showered their eulogies.

The desire to engrave haunted Blake like a passion. It would seem as though he had discovered a new sense. His mind and, as always where Blake is concerned, his heart and his soul, are wholly absorbed in his engraver's work. Suddenly without any warning, sorrow descends upon him. His brother of whom he was so fond, dies at his side. Blake is heartbroken. He calls upon the name of the dead, he sadly invokes his memory. And now behold, while he is seeking to forget his sorrow in strenuous toil, his brother comes to him and leads him to the discovery of new secrets in the engraver's art. The spirit of his brother Robert counselled him to give up engraving as he had been taught and in future to engrave the white and not the black. And this henceforth, was the method adopted by Blake.

III. *The years of strife* (1788-1811)

It is important to know, when we are studying this period of Blake's work, that, at this time, he was a poet as well as an engraver. That is to say, without giving up engraving as a means of expressing the soul within him, he felt as it were driven to write verses. It is even alleged that he sang his poems to airs of his own composition which unfortunately were never noted down. Blake lived intensely, and, obedient to the lash of his genius, he sought by every possible means to give the fullest expression to the soul within him. Of course this did not come about by chance and all at once, this new mode of self-expression. No doubt from the days when he was a child and all the time he was growing to manhood, he had been seeking other ways to unburden his spirit, but it was now above all that he realised to the full the inadequacy of one art taken alone, and the limitations of art as a whole.

This poetic outburst throws an instructive light on the lyrical quality of his engravings. It was impossible for Blake to chain himself down to elaborate some detail, impossible to curb his ardour, and this it is that explains, better than the comments of all critics, the effect upon Blake of external influences. For example, he has often been reproached with having appropriated certain faces, certain elements, in the work of Michael Angelo. Knowing the mind of Blake, we can easily see that, filled with admiration for Michael Angelo, he would rather have laid hands on what he wanted boldly and without concealment, than have endeavoured hypocritically to dissemble his action. Let us remember, as we look on certain engravings that inevitably recall Michael Angelo, what André

Gide has said « Those who are afraid of being influenced by others, make tacit avowal of their own poverty of soul ».

Viewed in this light, the pictures in which external influence is most evident, be it the influence of Michael Angelo, or the Gothic sculptors, will appear to us as the most perfect manifestations of his poetic spirit.

Being master of his craft, and that craft most personal in character, Blake refused to have recourse to the usual professional artifices. Rather his aim was to set himself free and to make the art of engraving a direct and not a second-hand one, if one may so express it.

The first important book which Blake was commissioned to illustrate was the *Night Thoughts* of Edward Young, a work which, at this period, was enjoying an immense popularity, but which, despite its undoubted beauty, has since fallen into undeserved neglect. There was, indeed, no special fitness in this coming together of Blake and Young. Blake's poetic gift and Young's have nothing in common save greatness. But the study of the book had the effect of confirming Blake in his ideas.

We may see from other illustrated editions of Young's *Night Thoughts* what sort of passages usually tempted the engraver. A comparison of their work with Blake's helps us to get an insight into the latter's idea of his art. In interpreting *Night Thoughts* he deliberately abstained from illustrating the text. And we may note the enormous difference which sunders the art of the illustrator from that of the engraver as Blake conceived it. In his view it was the function of engravings to complete the text, nay he went futrher and deemed that they might add to and extend it. Whereas with an illustrator all he had to do was to emphasise certain passages in the book which owe their choice not to their intrinsic importance but to the readiness with which they lend themselves to picturesque treatment. The engraver, according to Blake's idea, considers the work as a whole and proceeds from the particular to the general. It is his business to capture the very essence of it ; whereas the illustrator is content to lay stress on some pretty or « amusing » detail. The two things differ both in letter and in spirit.

Blake's ambition went far beyond all that. He endeavoured to transpose Young's poem into the realm of a plastic art, and each engraving reflects the style and movement of the poem. It is, incidentally, a thing worthy of remark and admiration that Blake, living as he did at the end of the Eighteenth Century, when the illustrations of the younger Moreau for example were looked upon with so much favour, should have been so profoundly impressed with what we may call the fallacy of the age. Nor need we wonder that, save for a few rare exceptions, his conception of the engraver's art should have met with indignation or ridicule.

It must none the less be recognised, after studying the engravings in Young's poem, that Blake was cramped and handicapped by being more or less tied down to the text. Blake must needs use his imagination, and, when his imagination is fettered, we are immediately and at a glance, aware of the sort of distress that numbs his efforts. Considered technically Blake's engravings to Young's *Night Thoughts* are remarkable, but they convey an impression of constraint. Blake needed to conceive his subject and visualise his engraving at the same time. He created a whole world of his own.

Aided first by Lavater and then by Swedenborg, he set forth on the discovery of another world as different as possible from this terrestrial globe. What kind of a world this was we may discover for ourselves, thanks to the work which some consider his greatest achievement, namely, *The Marriage of Heaven and Hell.*

When we examine the engravings which date from the beginning of this period, we cannot distinguish any general line.

They are manifestly works due to sudden inspiration or to exaltation and it is hardly possible to do more than note certain points of resemblance that would seem common to them all. Possibly the general movement which in many cases we might call their *élan* is a trait in common ; nevertheless their inequality is obvious.

One of the most characteristic productions of this period and indeed of Blake's work in general, is the picture entitled, *Nelson guiding Leviathian*. Here we may note at once the influence of Michael Angelo and the Gothic sculptors, which had affected him more profoundly than any other hitherto. The figures are at once demoniacal and titanic. Nelson, in the centre, recalls *Saint Michael overcoming the Dragon,* and some portions of the frescoes in the Sixtine chapel.

When the effect of these resemblances has worn off we are impressed by its imaginative power and not only by that sense of motion which we are tempted to call perpetual, but above all, by that kind of fury which suggests the wild leaping up of flames of fire. When Blake would depict the Infernal Regions, as is here the case, he does not try to suggest by terrifying details or by means of analogies and contrasts, he trusts rather to atmosphere, to a sudden unfolding of the whole. It is not a number of flames that he makes us see, but one flame, single and swift.

A few years earlier, in 1793, he had engraved those weird runes which describe one of the visions of the Daughters of Albion. There we have the same glorious uprising, the same grandeur of form, and, since they are in some sort a poetic commentary on this picture, they may be quoted here :

Then Oothoon waited silent all the day and all the night ;
But when the morning arose, her lamentations renewed.
The Daughters of Albion hear her woes and eccho back her sighs.

O Urizen! Creator of men! mistaken Demon of heaven!

Thy joys are tears, thy labours vain to form men to thine image.
How can one joy absorb another? are not different joys
Holy, eternal, infinite? and each joy is a Love.

Does not the great mouth laugh at a gift & the narrow eyelids mock
At the labour that is above payment? and wilt thou take the ape
For thy councellor, or the dog for a schoolmaster to thy children?
Does he who contemns poverty and he who turns with abhorrence
From usury feel the same passion or are they moved alike?
How can the giver of gifts experience the delights of the merchant?
How the industrious citizen the pains of the husbandman?
How different far the fat fed hireling with the hollow drum,
Who buys whole cornfields into wastes and sings upon the heath!

. . . . must chilling murderous thoughts obscure
The clear heaven of her eternal spring ; to bear the wintry rage
Of a harsh terror, driven to madness, bound to hold a rod
Over her shrinking shoulders all the day & all the night
To turn the wheel of false desire, and longings that wake her womb
To the abhorred birth of cherubs in the human form,
That live a pestilence and die a meteor, and are no more ;
Till the child dwell with one he hates, and do the deed he loaths,
And the impure scourge force his seed into its unripe birth
Ere yet his eyelids can behold the arrows of the day?

The same « spirit » broods over this invocation, and the picture of *Nelson guiding Leviathan* is a reflexion of the same light. In the case of all Blake's most famous pictures we may try a similar experiment and place a poem and a picture side by side. A criticism that may with some measure of justice be levelled at Blake's engravings is that most of them were composed after the manner of poems. At the same time it must be allowed that these poems possess a power which prompts us to liken them to visions. What gives this impression is that Blake depicts the *ensemble*, the whole field, the wide domain, but tends to neglect details. Faces, for example, never interested Blake. In none of his pictures does he ever insist on a precise detail, and least of all on the details of his faces. He distributes an equality of values over the whole. As for faces, so for hands. He never lays stress on the hands of his figures.

All his interest, all his enthusiasm, is centred in attitudes, in movement, for on these things he may look as indexes of the will. Purely human psychology has but a secondary interest for him. If we scrutinise with close attention the plates in Young's *Night Thoughts* we find ourselves brought face to face with problems which aim at something transcending human art and in which human psychology necessary plays no part. For Blake, soul and mind do not stand for something that may be dissected, for something we may take to pieces, like a machine. When he brings his mind to bear on them, it is in order to peer into their essence or their destiny, not to find out how, or of what, they are made. This remark, which would shew Blake's disdain for psychology, might with equal justice be made concerning everything he regarded as a restriction or a habit.

In another work of his, *Naomi and Ruth*, a work of equal importance, we may, though here the phenomenon is less conspicuous, discern what we may call the consequences of the miracle. At first sight this composition seems more « anecdotic », but on closer examination the same strange power becomes manifest, the mere story fades away leaving behind it the atmosphere, the lyrical essence, which are its most precious parts. It is in the picture as a whole that the power resides and not in any one section considered apart from the rest. In *Naomi and Ruth*, the tall draped female figures when detached do not even leave a gap. We cannot praise in Blake, as we usually can in a painter who knows his business, the sort of skill which consists in an effective *mise en page*, in putting things in their due position, or in the accurate observance of certain geometrical laws.Blake's skill is not there (he himself said it was not of this world) because his aim and desire are not the aim and desire of other painters.

Laurence Binyon, ingeniously remarks that Blake's work seems to loom larger and to gain in beauty when we contemplate the images left by it in our memory, so that it often happens that we experience a feeling of disappointment when we look again at the actual picture. His work, says Laurence Binyon, exerts a greater power on the mind than on the eye. That, it would seem, is a thing which Blake himself said when he declared that one should look « through one's eyes ».

Blake's art, whereof we may now recognise not only the power but the inward spirit, does not admit of being judged by the canons we apply to the general run of artists. This is a point to be borne in mind, we must indeed never lose sight of it, lest misunderstanding should lead to misjudgment. We must consider it as a province of the artist's life, of which it was never more than a manifestation, and, we must contemplate it in that particular aspect to which we may perhaps apply the therm « miraculous ». If we endeavoured further to analyse the essence of his genius we should soon founder on some such reef as « pure art » or, « pure poetry ».

It was never in Blake's mind to provide us with the solution to a problem of this nature. In his poems and particularly in his *Descriptive Catalogue* his sole aim was, not to explain, but to transfigure. He merely tells us that his world is not our world.

« The Prophets », he says, « describe what they saw in vision as real and existing men whom they saw with their imaginative and immortal organs ; the Apostles the same ; the clearer the organ, the more distinct the object. A spirit and a vision are not, as the modern philosophy supposes, a cloudy vapour or a nothing : they are organised and minutely articulated beyond all that the mortal and perishing nature can produce. He who does not imagine in stronger and better lineaments, and in stronger and better light, than his perishing mortal eye can see, does not imagine at all. The painter of this work asserts that all his imaginations appear to him infinitely more perfect and more minutely organised than anything seen by his mortal eye. »

The *Descriptive Catalogue* is dated 1809, the year of Blake's supreme effort, the year in which he reaches the zenith of his powers. Totally and universally misunderstood, Blake, now full master of his art and assured of his vision, resolves to make yet one more attempt to reveal to the world the truth within him. The attempt was made in vain, but his voice has come to us and we must give heed to it, not to admire but, at long last, to admit, the significance of his message. For Blake never courted admiration, never sought to make acquaintance with glory ; but strove with passionate insistence to disperse the misunderstandings by which his art was, as it were, hid from view.

At the end of this year 1809, after the glaring failure of his exhibition and the ridicule which greeted the appearance of his *Descriptive Catalogue,* Blake's attitude enlightens us as to his past intentions. When he became quite convinced that no one in this world, save the woman at his side, could enter into the world which he desired to make known to mankind and to which he offered to serve them as a guide, then, at last, without hesitation, he ceased to paint, to write or to sing. He kept a stubborn silence. His engravings, as well as his poems, were, then, nought but gleams whose ray would vouchsafe us a glimpse of another world. Their significance was no matter of aesthetic beauty, but a kind of revelation.

And then, later on, after years of silence and total inactivity, when there came to him men who fain to follow him as their guide, Blake never wavered an instant. He resumed his task and a new era, an active and fruitful era was begun.

IV. *Years of obscurity* (1811-1817)

English critics of Blake's work as an engraver have always sought, perhaps unwittingly, for reasons outside that work itself, to justify their praise and admiration of it. They tried, because they loved it, to link it up with the work of his predecessors, and to assign it a niche in the world of space and time.

It would seem however that what is most admirable in these engravings is that their aspect and intention are deliberately divorced from space and time.

While, on the one hand, Blake strove to set himself free, others did their utmost to bind him faster than ever. The sole effort which Blake essayed to hold communion with his contemporaries, I mean his *Descriptive Catalogue*, met with a decided reverse. This catalogue however may be studied with profit, for it definitely enlightens us not only on his mode of work but on its inspiration. Blake returns again and again, in connexion with nearly all his engravings, to the necessity of looking not *with* our eyes, but *through* our eyes ; in other words he enjoins us to seek the imaginative import of a work and not merely a pleasurable sensation. Every one of Blake's pictures is a theme for meditation, a sort of framework in which the mind, the spirit, must move and have its being with the greatest possible intensity. Thus Blake did not look upon his pictures as works of art, that is to say as ornaments, but placed them on a plane exclusively spiritual. It is of small importance that Blake, as was his custom, took his examples from the Bible and, in order to make himself the better understood, laid stress on the authority and universal appeal of that book ; the truly remarkable thing about the *Descriptive Catalogue* is its lucidity. It was not chance, it was not will, that compelled Blake to choose his subjects and to adopt a certain technique. He manifests his astonishment at being so different, so remote from his contemporaries. With a humility that resembles *naïveté* — but only resembles it — Blake presents his pictures to the world, declaring that they must not be looked upon as works of art but as sketches, adumbrations of vivions. « Here », he seems to say to us, « is a representation, imperfect indeed, of what I have seen, and what I have seen is worthy of admiration. Never will any picture of mine be able to give you an idea thereof. » And he requests the spectator to join in with him, he tries to guides him, to point out to him how it behoves him to use his eyes. If we examine any of his pictures attentively, we shall see that, despite its finished appearance, everything is merely hinted at and that it is the beholder's business to follow out these indications in his own mind.

This teaching was not understood and it may afford matter for astonishment that, even in our own day, people still refuse to give consideration to the counsels of a man who could boast of such lucidity as Blake could in this particular case.

These « years of obscurity », notwithstanding their complete sterility, may, nevertheless, be looked upon as necessary. Blake's poetic state of mind enveloped him in a deep shadow. He began by feeling a need to exhibit his work, and to comment upon it. Then he must needs cease this exhausting labour of engraving. And with equal fervour he flings himself into silence.

These years of silent inactivity might have sundered Blake from everything to which we give the name of art. If Blake, weary of his task, had given up all idea of work, people might have invented as they did in Arthur Rimbaud's case, some sort of culpable surrender and have given out that Blake had admitted the futility of his work. But one of the remarkable things about is the serenity with which he resumed his task after these barren years, and the fact that these later works are more perfectly finished than those which he exhibited in 1809.

It is likely enough that during those long years, when the world was nothing to him and he nothing to the world, Blake never really completely gave up work. It is open to us to suppose that he pondered upon his pictures, that he meditated upon the works of his hands. Perhaps it sufficed him to bethink himself of the flame which had inspired him, in order to recapture, in the contemplation of his pictures, the same exaltation and the same vision. It is absurd to suppose that Blake stopped the working of his mind in a single day. He merely ceased to produce, to manifest himself, to turn his countenance to the world, and to entrust to the verdict of men that which he deemed a work divine, whereof he declared that he was not the author, only claiming to interpret the will of a lofty and superhuman genius.

The silence of the outer world which enveloped Blake at this period of his life had a pronounced effect upon his work. When he resumed his labours he endeavoured to find calmness and to turn his lyrical passion inwards, if one may so put it. One would imagine that during these years, the thoughts of Blake dwelt long upon death and on the peace which comes with it. At the outset of his career, when he was copying the tombs in Westminster Abbey, and, later, when he was asked to supply engravings for Blair's *The Grave*, his work compelled him to meditate on death. And if, as to-day we can, we bethink ourselves of all that romanticism, after the Middle Ages, read into man's end, of all the tragi-comic paraphernalia with which death was bedizened in those times, we cannot but marvel at the lucidity and, still more, at the serenity with which Blake withstood the conceptions of the past ages, of his own day, and even of the future.

In his lonely old age, with Eternity, a glowing reality, before his eyes, Blake neither jeered nor trembled, nor did he cheat himself with illusions. Rather did he take on a serenity which was, as it were, a promise of that unruffled calm with which he afterwards came to face his end, or as he preferred to call it, his departure. When it fell to him to depict a death scene, he created the same atmosphere as he would employ for a birth, and such pictures derive from this simplicity of soul, a depth of meaning, a profound significance, which far transcends in interest the technical skill with which they are wrought.

During these « obscure years » Blake acquired a new character which imparted to the work of the concluding period of his life a strength and a distinction possessed by none of the pictures he had produced hitherto.

V. *The Happy Years* (1817-1827)

After his strenuous labours, Blake immured himself in the profoundest silence, resolved it would seem to let Death come to him, and, while waiting for its summons, to range in solitude that universe which he had, long since, endeavoured to make known to his fellows.

We know absolutely nothing of those six years, and Blake never referred to that period of his life. It never occurred to him to explain or to justify his renunciation. All we know is that in 1812, as if in defiance of past verdicts, he added some fresh touches to his great picture *The Prologue and Characters of Chaucer's Pilgrims*. It was because this picture so completely failed to be understood that Blake decided he would work no more.

And then Cumberland first of all, next Linnel and finally Varley went to see him. Their friendship and enthusiasm comforted him and he resolved to set to work anew. But a change had come over him, a change in his attitude towards the world which, when we remember the fire and the fury of his fighting days, may strike us as singular. Blake is described for us by the people with whom he came in contact at this time, as a good sterling fellow, simple, gentle, indulgent and *in the clouds*. This was not the man who hurled defiance at public opinion and walked about the London streets with a red cap of liberty on his head ; this was not the whole-hearted admirer and champion of the French Revolution. Blake's sweetness and indulgence disarmed those who came to jeer at his visions and the laughter died on their lips. When he calmly began to talk of his conversation with Milton or Dante, he did it with such utter simplicity, that no one dared suspect his sincerity.

After his long period of retirement it was more and more as a visionary that Blake appeared to the world. He gave up explaining his visions as he had done in his *Descriptive Catalogue*, in which he endeavoured, as it were, to give them a human character, but he spoke about them in the simplest manner in the world, heedless of the mockers and the sceptics.

Blake was indeed like a man enslaved by his visions. All his pictures have the energy of a sudden conflagration that follows a period of meditation. A passage whether it were culled from the Book of Job, or from Dante or even Virgil, was but a pretext. More often than not his visions came to Blake, spontaneously, unsolicited. This his friend Varley the painter was sympathetic and clearsighted enough to perceive.

It seems to me futile to « consider too curiously », as all his biographers appear to me to do, the nature of these visions of his and to attach such tremendous importance to deciding whether or not Blake really saw the things he described and put into pictures. I should have thought it more profitable to seek to appreciate in his pictures the real beauty and power which this « method » of his imparted to them.

What impresses one in the pictures that belong to Blake's period of maturity is a sense of perfection which his earlier work did not convey.

A change had come over Blake. There had been a time when he was impatient of « finicking » with his work. Now, no trouble was too great to produce the most consummate finish. All the engravings in the *Book of Job*, which are among the most popular of his works, are executed with minute precision, and every one of the numerous and tiny details is treated with the most elaborate care.

The quantity of drawings which Blake made for these engravings shew the great importance he attached to technical perfection. But when, after paying the first spontaneous tribute of admiration, we come to look into the engravings, we find ourselves in the presence ot the same poetic inspiration. In my opinion, however. Blake was harassed and constrained by technical preoccupations, and most of these plates make us look back with longing to the freedom of his earlier work. We are now forced to realise that Blake was an old man and that his hand had lost some of the firmness of earlier days. But what compels our admiration is the longevity of his poetic genius which, despite advancing age, despite meticulous attention to details, bore him irresistibly onwards and exalted him above the things of earth. Blake in his old age was essentially the same as he had always been, yet differing from that earlier self which had acknowledged no other rule than the wave of his own enthusiasm. Having resolved to illustrate the *Divina Commedia*, he set himself to re-read the poem. Dissatisfied with the translation, he learnt Italian in order that he might read Dante's own words. Such preoccupations prove that Blake was, in some measure, desirous of verifying his own visions. His drawings for the *Divina Commedia* are the most generally admired of all his work. Their power and the perfection of their workmanship are indeed amazing, but they are valuable also in another way, for, whereas all Dante's other illustrators are occupied with incidents, with stories, Blake makes no attempt to illustrate these things. He is occupied only with those parts of the poem in which its spiritual significance is most clearly manifested. Blake's illustrations are presentments of the spiritual essence. Not because he shunned figures as such, but because the abstracted essence was more moving, in his eyes, more inspiring, than the goings and comings of the characters. This 'abstraction' became a matter of vision. The story runs that Blake on seeing a thistle said :

> For a double vision my eyes do see,
> And a double vision is always with me.
> With my inward eyes 'tis an old man grey
> With my outward, a thistle across my way.

It was not only the thistle that suggested such reflections to Blake. He could deliver himself of similar declarations when he encountered on his way the idea of Liberty for example, for he sees it internally and externally. And all the drawings for the *Divina Commedia* are confirmations of this faculty.

When Blake took to his bed for the last time, he was working on a large painting of which the subject was *The Last Judgment*. This picture was lost, but it may afford matter for astonishment that a dying man should be in sufficient possession of his faculties to strive passionately to prefigure the things with which he deemed he would soon be face to face. It was while giving proof of his strength that Blake breathed his last. By this final gesture, he refuted the arguments of those who held that he was mad or at all events brainsick. Of course it cannot be denied that there was something apocalyptic in Blake's composition and that his genius shook him so fiercely that his works are at once tumultuous, disjointed and unequal; but it must also be recognised — and this is what I have endeavoured to emphasise in this work — that Blake, if he was sometimes dominated by his visions, as soon as be became conscious of his « superhuman » power, succeeded in giving his works an incomparable *élan* and in putting them outside those rules which tend to make of painting, and more especially of engraving, an uninspired and vulgar art, a mere matter of imitation and decoration.

If we are to do full justice to William Blake we must bear in mind that, in his day, it required great courage and a rare power, thus resolutely to turn aside from the beaten track. Blake's life, so full of suffering, sometimes tragic in its intensity, shows all too clearly that one cannot leave the common highway with impunity. « Mad Blake », the lunatic engraver, the sorry creature, was impelled to think and to meditate aloof from his own times, and we know that to do this voluntarily or involuntarily, a man must be upborne by the power of ge-

nius. It must also be borne in mind that his achievement, by
the loftiness of its design, is of the kind that leaves on the mind
an ineffaceable imprint. And further, since Blake is an engraver, we must also recognise that the example he set was the
means of restoring its *raison d'être*, its autonomy, if one may so
put it, to the engraver's art, by breaking with the routine of
the Eighteenth Century which made this branch of the Fine
Arts purely and simply a medium of reproduction.

It is only here and there that I have laid stress on the « extraordinary » side of Blake's work, for I hold that to do so is
to distort its significance. Blake owes a part of his « vogue »
to-day to the fact that the critics hold him up as a phenomenon
and express amazement that, although he never left England,
some of the figures in his pictures recall the religious carvings
of India. Many of his admirers, and the majority of his com-
mentators, look upon him as a sort of medium and with that
zealous faith which spiritualists commonly display, will suffer
no discussion of his works and ideas.

But the problem to which the life and works of William
Blake give rise are of a nature more human, and notwithstanding that, perhaps more mysterious. Blake as an artist and as
a man, comes before us as the genius, with his fine frenzies, his
outbursts, his sudden swoopings, his famous flashes, his blind
gropings and his wonderful gleams of radiant light.

Judged by the canons we should apply to any artist of
talent, Blake may prove disappointing, for he no more aims at
exciting pleasure or emotion than he aims at presenting us
with a work of art. We know that Blake was a great poet, and
we must always remember when we are looking at a picture
by him that he executed it like a poem. Not by any means that
I wish to limit the admiration one may feel for Blake's engravings to what we are accustomed to call their « literary » side.
Quite the contrary, for this side of his work, having often been
imposed on him from without, is devoid of any great interest.

But Blake's pictures are possessed of that absolute, or, as we may put it, gratuitous character, which is generally conceded to poetry.

Mr Arthur Symons, in his monograph on Blake, probably the most remarkable work on the subject, gives a magnificient description of Blake's attitude.

« The mind of Blake lay open to Eternity as a seed plot lies open to the sower. In 1802 he writes to Mr Butts from Felpham : 'I am not ashamed, afraid or averse to tell you what ought to be told, that I am under the direction of messengers from heaven, daily and nightly' — 'I have written this poem', he says of the *Jerusalem*, 'from immediate dictation, twelve or sometimes twenty or thirty lines at a time, without premeditation, and even against my will.' 'I may praise it,' he says in another letter, 'since I dare not pretend to be any other than the secretary, the authors are in Eternity.'

« In these words, the most precise claim for direct inspiration which Blake ever made, there is nothing different in kind, only in degree, from what must be felt by every really creative artist and by every profoundly and simply religious person. There can hardly be a poet who is not conscious of how little his own highest powers are under his own control. The creation of beauty is the end of art, but the artist should rarely admit to himself that such is his purpose. A poem is not written by the man who says : I will sit down and write a poem ; but rather by the man who, captured by, rather than capturing, an impulse, hears a tune which he does not recognise, or sees a sight which he does not remember, in some 'close corner of his brain' and exerts the only energy at his disposal in recording it faithfully, in the medium of his particular art. And so in every creation of beauty, some obscure desire stirred in the soul, not realised by the mind for what it was, and, aiming at most other things in the world than pure beauty, produced it. »

By his life and work Blake reveals to us the power and in some sort, the infallibility of this faculty.

It is not without advantage that time, as it were, fixed a gulf between Blake and all his contemporaries. It was becoming that his art should escape the hasty eulogies, and the misjudgments that are the products of a lack of recoil. It was necessary that a century should pass by so that it might be looked at from a distance and its true greatness summed up. This interval of time enables us to view it in its true perspective.

That Blake should not be generally popular is easily understood when we bear in mind that it never occurred to him to play to the gallery. He was profoundly imbued with a feeling for grandeur. First and foremost he would have it that his art was something higher than anything he had been taught about it and he refused to look upon it as a mere craft. He put it on so high a pedestal as to claim that what he did was not due to him, in his human capacity, and that he was nothing more than the instrument of everlasting forces. When Blake is called upon to choose it is always to things on high that he directs his vision. Eternity is his goal.

« Imagination », he exclaims, « is the real and eternal world of which this vegetable universe is but a faint shadow, and in it we shall live in our eternal or imaginative bodies, when these vegetable mortal bodies are no more. »

Here it may not be unprofitable to emphasise that Blake drew the inspiration for nearly all his pictures from the Bible, from Milton's *Paradise Lost*, from the *Divina Commedia* or from some striking event of his own day, and never from that Graeco-Latin culture which, after the Middle Ages, was the fertilising principle of all art and the fountain of inspiration for all artists. But it was the Bible in particular that exerted upon Blake not merely a moral, but a plastic, influence. It was no mere chance that put it into his head to illustrate *The Book of Job,* in which we may find the grandeur and tragic simplicity of the majority of his pictures.

Passages like the following,

Let the day perish wherein I was born, and the night in which it was said, There is a man child conceived.

Let that day be darkness ; let not God regard it from above, neither let the light shine upon it.

Let darkness and the shadow of death stain it ; let a cloud dwell upon it ; let the blackness of the day terrify it.

call to our vision the black and white of those great scenes in which Blake shows us the battle between Day and Night, where black and white engage in deadly combat and are rent asunder.

Blake had been one of the earliest to recognise the truth contained in a dictum afterwards pronounced by Ernest Renan, the force of which Renan tempers with a note of interrogation.

« If we take a general view of the development of the Hebrew mind, we are struck by that lofty note of absolute perfection which gives the fruits of it the right to be regarded as classics, in the same way as the products of Greece and Rome and the peoples of Latin blood. Alone among all the races of the East, Israel was granted the privilege of writing for the entire world. There are certainly many admirable qualities in the poetry of the Vedas, and yet this sheaf of the early songs of the race to which we belong, will, in the utterance of our religious feelings, never take the place of the Psalms, those songs of a race so different from ours. The other literatures of the East can only be read and appreciated by scholars ; the literature of the Hebrews is the Bible, the Book of Books, wherein all mankind may read. Millions of men scattered over the face of the wide world know no other poetry than that of the

Bible. No doubt in taking stock of this amazing destiny we must make allowance for the religious revolutions which, in the sixteenth century in particular, brought men to look upon the Hebrew scriptures as the one and only source of revelation. But it may be affirmed that if these books had not contained something profoundly universal in character, they would never have met with that fortune. »

No doubt this comment of Renan's is profoundly true, yet it may reasonably be added that this very universality of the Book of Books and the perpetual reading of it, have worn away some of its grandeur and its beauty. We repeat its phrases, we say them over and over again like the burden of a song, and in the process we despoil them of some of their power. Blake, who was brought up on the Bible, was conscious, despite all this, of its amazing freshness and derived from it his incomparable power. Not only its beauty, not only its tragic significance did he make his own, but its sublime spirit he received into his very soul. Moreover it seems to be in the nature of things that Blake should have had this deep love of the Bible and have made it his constant source of inspiration, for the conception that came to him earliest and most readily was the conception of the sublime. He had, so to speak, a feeling for it and appeared naturally to cast aside whatever seemed calculated to bear him away from it, for he was not of those who can make the best of both worlds. The sublime bathes, so to speak, all his work and permeates its very essence. As a rule such continual striving after what is great and sublime is apt to weary in the long run and grandeur in an artist and particularly in an engraver runs the risk of degenerating into the grandiose. But with Blake, this loftiness is so much part of his being that age could not weary nor custom stale its varied manifestations. It was the kingdom in which he dwelt.

As Mr Arthur Symons so truly observes « Throughout his life his desire had been, as he said, to converse with his friends in Eternity see visions, dream dreams, and prophesy and speak parables unheard. »

> .... I rest not from my great task
> To open the Eternal worlds, to open the immortal eyes
> Of Man inwards into the worlds of thought, into Eternity
> Ever expanding in the bosom of God, the human imagination.

Such throughout his life was Blake's creed. He never changed his faith.

One might have expected that, in the long run, an artist thus given to contemplating the sublime would sooner or later be drawn to look upon the obverse of the medal, to the horrible or the terrifying. Even the most tragic of his compositions never convey the remotest suggestion of what we may call the romanticism of horror. So far was he from entertaining any such taste as that, that he even restored Satan to his pride of place. The explanation of *The Marriage of Heaven and Hell* with which Monsieur Pierre Berger inaugurates his translation, shows us that Blake exalted Hell and raised it to the category of the sublime.

« The main theory » (of *The Marriage of Heaven and Hell*) writes Monsieur Pierre Berger, « is that Hell consists of human energies represented by demons, and good in themselves; while Heaven means submission to factitious restrictions, to tyrannical laws, bad in themselves, but administered and observed by the Angels who represent the spirit of obedience and servitude. Swedenborg did not behold Truth in its entirety, for he only asked counsel of the angels, who deceived him. Blake looked upon the demons and the sight led him to turn the angels to derision. He ranges himself on the side of the demons, by which we are to understand the Instincts and Energies, against the Laws. But he declares that both are necessary, because without the two contraries there would be neither progress nor life. This reconcilling of the two opposing tendencies is the *Marriage*. Throughout the whole work, the successive visions must clearly be taken in a figurative sense. Blake believed in the real existence of everything that he imagined, and thus it is that he came to hold converse with Isaiah and Ezekiel and with the Demon, who became one of his friends. Everywhere we must be on the look out for these allegories and metaphors, for they are of frequent occurrence. The mills for example in which thoughts are ground and re-ground are the logical apparatus of debates and treatises. Then we have the precipices of doubt and error ; the flames of Creation, and Passion and Genius ; the tigers of mighty and manifold passions ; the steeds of wisdom and passive obedience (1). »

Blake's imagination brings before him pictorially the details of a world of his own, a world in which, all his life long, he was to move and have his being. His pictures and even his Visions were more real to him than the tangible world about him. The vigour of imagination empowered him to set the sublime above the terrestrial and, in a measure, to dwell in it. When Blake adumbrates his great theories and then proceeds to look on them as established truths, almost as revelations, he is in no way astonished at the religious atmosphere that envelopes them and is lost in almost childlike wonder at their sublimity. And when he completes a picture, his attitude is the same. An engraving too, is a truth and a revelation. Moreover there is but a negligible difference between the Blake who talks about the precipices of doubt and error, and the Blake who engraves plates for the Book of Job.

That unity of spirit which is made manifest alike in his poems and his engravings is summed up in his aspirations towards the sublime.

It is therefore proper to state that Blake never had, strictly speaking, any influence and that it is extremely probable that

---

(1) Pierre Berger, *Premiers livres prophétiques* (Les éditions Rieder).

he never will. The reason is that in Blake we behold not so much a fountain, a source, as a mountain top ; it is because he gathers up, as it were, within his own being the loftiest and the rarest aspirations of the noblest of mankind. And strange as it may seem, he was quite conscious that his art and his personality were sundered by a profound gulf from the spirit of his own time. Quite naturally, in the true painter's manner, he masks his affirmations, and being an engraver he clothes them. There is more than a little accuracy in this remark of Swinburne's :

« There are », he writes, « two points in the work of Blake which first claim notice and explanation, two points connected but not inseparable, his mysticism and his mythology. The latter is in fact hardly more, in its relation to the former, than the clothes to the body, or the body to the soul. To make either comprehensible it is requisite above all things to get sight of the man in whom they became incarnate and active as forces or as opinions. »

Blake, in fact, never tried to make himself understood. Marcel Brion (1) observes that Blake « lived a supernatural life, on an unknown plane, while, at the same time, his earthly existence flowed on without accident without those external events which sometimes change the current of a genius. His soul dwelt among the poets and prophets of old not in any metaphorical sense or through the medium of their works, but *directly*, by virtue of those subtle links which bind soul to soul. We may indeed say with truth that he dwelt in closer union with the people of his visions than with the actual men and women of the world about him. »

His work was bound to be looked on as a closed book, to appear obscure and incomprehensible. And when, even now, notwithstanding the light thrown upon it by critics and poets,

---

(1) *Navire d'argent*, n° 4.

we come to examine his pictures, we cannot help feeling sur-
prised at the impression we experience. Far from being char-
med by them, we are forced to the conclusion that they are
beyond the pale of admiration and that viewed merely as an
artist, Blake may prove disappointing. But if we cease to oc-
cupy ourselves with such things as charm and virtuosity, we
cannot fall to be struck with an art so exceptional as to lie
beyond the reach of admiration and criticism, as being of the
stuff that dreams are made on, noble yet childlike. And thus
it naturally came about that Blake, guided by his imagination
and dominated by his consciousness of the Eternal, all through
his life preferred the company of children to that of grown-up
men and women.

But since the encomiums of some of his admirers have, as it
were, invited a comparison of Blake with the general run of
engravers, it will not be amiss to assess his position among
them and to endeavour to anticipate misapprehensions by
explaining what it is he has to give us and what, in a human,
mundane sense, is the significance of his message.

Blake's work, though not to be praised or dispraised according to the generally accepted artistic canons, furnishes us,
with a conspicuous example of the power of art. No one in the
world was so fully conscious of the limitations of art as Blake.
But if he persevered, despite all the admonitions « from above »,
enjoining him to hold his peace, it was because he knew that
these engravings of his, the outcome of painful and exacting
toil, constituted a sort of currency, a sort of vehicle of ex-
change. In a sphere higher than that of what we call talent,
and even beyond the domain of genius, Blake strove to fulfil
a task, a mission, that should justify his life and his endea-
vours. Such a mission certainly had not for its object to bring
him into closer relationship with his fellow men, to help them,
or to enlighten them, but aimed rather at shunning their contact. And when, disgusted with their clumsy ridicule and igno-

rant misunderstanding, Blake resolved to lay aside his tools and work no more, he did so without repining, and lived on in the hope of silence. And he called on those friends who had never failed him to sustain him in a different task. Mankind interested him no more, and since his pictures gave offence, he ceased to exhibit and, by so doing, manifested his most profound conviction, the conviction that determined his activity or inactivity, the conviction that his real life was otherwhere than among his contemporaries, who were certainly far removed from the world of his dreams. But it must on no account be supposed that Blake looked down upon his fellow men. Scorn, in his eyes, was a weakness, perhaps the outcome of disappointment at not being appreciated or understood. William Blake never learnt disdain. Sometimes he hated, because he loved ; but he never descended to the level of those who mocked at him.

The opinions of his friends, the counsels of those who instructed him in his craft, had only a superficial effect upon him.

I cannot help comparing him to another artist who was also looked upon as mad, who was misrepresented no less than Blake, I mean that strange genius Paolo Uccello, one of the greatest and most misunderstood of Florentines. Towards the end of his life Uccello had definitely cut himself off from the world.

And so it was with Blake. He never succeeded in interesting himself in the world about him. In the lives of both these great men, of both these great visionaries, there is a like sense of destiny, a like grandeur. How could we fail to be struck with their common daring, or with the lack of comprehension with which their work was received. I believe that the cause of this profound misunderstanding resides in the fact that there is an almost complete incompatibility between the critics who, when all is said and done, do shape the judgment of the general run of folk, and consequently of posterity, and that poetry of the soul which animated Uccello and Blake in all their work. All the efforts one may make to understand, even dimly, such work as theirs, are inevitably restricted to a lower plane. With the best will in the world we cannot, by any ordinary mental process, measure the soul or sound its depths. Blake, when he was working on an engraving, seemed, so it has been said, to lose his wits, because he was as though scorched by an inward fire, and was careless of his workmanship, that is to say of all those time-honoured tricks devices which people are so pleased to recognise in paintings and engravings. When Blake set himself to carry out the behests which his spirit laid upon him, he ceased to heed the rules which his instructors and his friends had sought to fetter him. We are in danger of committing a still more egregious error to-day, if we prefer dissecting a picture by Blake, to experiencing the emotion, the shock of wonder to which the contemplation of it gives rise within us. Above that general average of performance which we may call everyday art, workaday art, some painters arise and stir up in us a belief in the supremacy of certain modes of expression, and we forget, then, that such artists are the exception and not the rule. Blake immediately impresses us by his simplicity, his facility and then by his submissiveness, all of which are as it were springes to ensnare our vanity. We take purity for simplicity. We are too ready to abstain from the effort we ought to have made if we had really beheld aright. In a word, to employ the phrase in vogue to-day, we may say that Blake is a « difficult » artist and all the more difficult because at first sight his work seems to suggest the quality of gentle, childlike simplicity. All the studies of Blake that have hitherto seen the light, are but introductory and, although they bear distinguished signatures, although they are the work of men renowned for their culture and their erudition and their delicate critical insight, they are nevertheless merely preliminary. For our part we crave indulgence for having sought, eagerly it is true, to shed a few gleams over Blake's work as an engraver, rather than to produce a general and popular monograph upon him. When Blake is in question, popularity must be put aside.

Blake had no wish for his work to be looked on as a pleasurable diversion. He valued respect at a higher rate than earthly fame. He looked for no recognition from the men and women of his time, because he attempted neither to shock nor to charm them. Nor had he any greater expectations from posterity. It mattered little to him that his work should perish. He wrought it with infinite pains, but without any clearly defined object. Probably he worked because his genius compelled him to work.

I believe that if admiration is his to-day, it is because he never courted admiration, because, if the truth must be told, he seemed to despise it. For many years to come, perhaps for ever, it will remain something apart, I mean it will only be really loved by the few.

We may be sure that lovers of Blake will at all times be rare, but they will be passionate lovers, for Blake's art is not of the kind that people argue about. They either hate it or love it, unquestioningly.

BIBLIOGRAPHICAL NOTE

LAURENCE BINYON. *The Drawings and Engravings of William Blake*. (London, 1922. The Studio.)

DARRELL FIGGIS. *The Paintings of William Blake*. (London, 1925. Benn.)

Gray's Poems illustrated by William Blake. (Oxford, University Press.)

Milton's Poems illustrated by William Blake. (London, 1926. The Nonesuch Press.)

ELLIS and YEATS. *The Works of William Blake*. (London, 1893, 3 vol. Quaritch.)

A. GILCHRIST. *Life of William Blake*. (London, 1863, 2 vol. republished in 1880 and in 1907.)

P. BERGER. *William Blake, Mysticisme et Poesie*. (Thèse de doctorat, 1907.)

P. BERGER. *Premiers livres prophétiques*, traduits de l'anglais avec une introduction (Paris, 1927. Les Éditions Rieder.)

PL. 3. DEATH ON THE PALE HORSE.
LA MORT SUR LE CHEVAL BLÊME.
TOD AUF FAHLEM PFERDE.
LA MORTE SUL CAVALLO PALLIDO.
LA MUERTE SOBRE EL CABALLO PALIDO.

PL. 4. ENGRAVING FOR YOUNG'S NIGHTS.
GRAVURE POUR LES NUITS DE YOUNG.
STICH FÜR YOUNGS « NÄCHTE ».
INTAGLIO PER LE NOTTI DI YOUNG.
GRABADO PARA LAS NOCHES DE YOUNG.

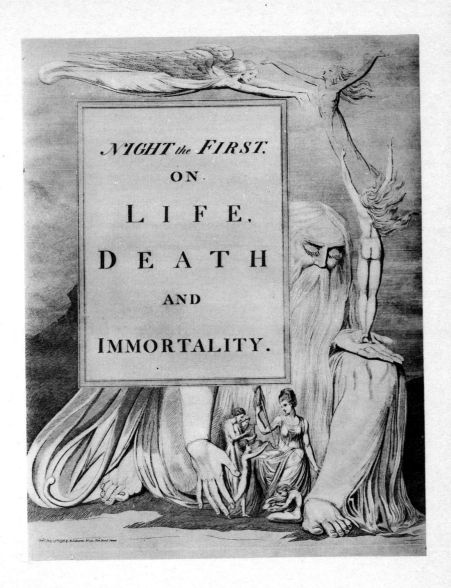

NIGHT the FIRST.

ON

LIFE,

DEATH

AND

IMMORTALITY.

PL. 5. ENGRAVING FOR YOUNG'S NIGHTS.
GRAVURE POUR LES NUITS DE YOUNG.
STICH FÜR YOUNGS « NÄCHTE ».
INTAGLIO PER LE NOTTI DI YOUNG.
GRABADO PARA LAS NOCHES DE YOUNG.

8

Bliss! sublunary bliss!—proud words, and vain!
Implicit treason to divine decree!
A bold invasion of the rights of heaven!
I clasp'd the phantoms, and I found them air:
O had I weigh'd it ere my fond embrace,
What darts of agony had miss'd my heart!
* Death! great proprietor of all! 'tis thine
To tread out empire, and to quench the stars:
The sun himself by thy permission shines;
And, one day, thou shalt pluck him from his sphere.
Amidst such mighty plunder, why exhaust
Thy partial quiver on a mark so mean?
Why thy peculiar rancour wreak'd on me?
Insatiate archer! could not one suffice?
Thy shaft flew thrice—and thrice my peace was slain;
And thrice, ere thrice yon moon had fill'd her horn.
O Cynthia! why so pale? dost thou lament
Thy wretched neighbour? grieve to see thy wheel
Of ceaseless change outwhirl'd in human life?
How wanes my borrow'd bliss from fortune's smile!
Precarious courtesy! not virtue's sure,
Self-given, solar ray of sound delight.

In every varied posture, place, and hour,
How widow'd every thought of every joy!
Thought, busy thought! too busy for my peace,
Through the dark postern of time long elapsed,
Led softly; by the stillness of the night,
Led like a murderer, and such it proves;
Strays, wretched rover! o'er the pleasing past;
In quest of wretchedness perversely strays;

PL. 6. ENGRAVING FOR YOUNG'S NIGHTS.
GRAVURE POUR LES NUITS DE YOUNG.
STICH FÜR YOUNGS « NÄCHTE ».
INTAGLIO PER LE NOTTI DI YOUNG.
GRABADO PARA LAS NOCHES DE YOUNG.

To naked waste; a dreary vale of tears:
The great magician's dead! thou poor pale piece
Of outcast earth—in darkness! what a change
From yesterday! thy darling hope so near,
Long-labour'd prize, O how ambition flush'd
Thy glowing cheek! ambition, truly great,
Of virtuous praise: death's subtle seed within,
Sly, treacherous miner! working in the dark,
Smiled at thy well-concerted scheme, and beckon'd
The worm to riot on that rose so red,
Unfaded ere it fell—one moment's prey!

    Man's foresight is conditionally wise;
LORENZO! wisdom into folly turns
Oft, the first instant its idea fair
To lab'ring thought is born: how dim our eye!
* The present moment terminates our sight;
Clouds, thick as those on doomsday, drown the next;
We penetrate, we prophesy in vain:
Time is dealt out by particles; and each,
Ere mingled with the streaming sands of life,
By fate's inviolable oath is sworn
Deep silence, " where eternity begins."

    By nature's law, what may be, may be now;
There's no prerogative in human hours:
In human hearts what bolder thought can rise,
Than man's presumption on to-morrow's dawn?
Where is to-morrow?—in another world!
For numbers this is certain; the reverse
Is sure to none; and yet on this perhaps,
This peradventure—infamous for lies,

PL. 7. ENGRAVING FOR YOUNG'S NIGHTS.
GRAVURE POUR LES NUITS DE YOUNG.
STICH FÜR YOUNGS « NÄCHTE ».
INTAGLIO PER LE NOTTI DI YOUNG.
GRABADO PARA LAS NOCHES DE YOUNG.

16

The sprightly lark's shrill matin wakes the morn,
Grief's sharpest thorn hard pressing on my breast:
I strive, with wakeful melody, to cheer
The sullen gloom, sweet philomel! like thee,
And call the stars to listen; every star
Is deaf to mine, enamour'd of thy lay:
Yet be not vain; there are, who thine excel,
And charm through distant ages: wrapp'd in shade,
Pris'ner of darkness! to the silent hours,
How often I repeat their rage divine,
To lull my griefs, and steal my heart from woe!
I roll their raptures, but not catch their fire:
Dark, though not blind, like thee Mæonides!
Or, Milton! thee; ah, could I reach your strain!
Or his, who made Mæonides our own:
Man too he sung—immortal man I sing:
* Oft bursts my song beyond the bounds of life;
What now, but immortality, can please?
O had he press'd his theme, pursued the track,
Which opens out of darkness into day!
O had he mounted on his wing of fire,
Soar'd, where I sink, and sung immortal man!
How had it bless'd mankind, and rescued me!

London Pub.ᵈ Aug.ᵗ 1ˢᵗ 1796 by R. Edwards, 142 New Bond Street.

Pregnant with all eternity can give ;
Pregnant with all that makes archangels smile:
Who murders time, he crushes in the birth
A power 'ethereal, only not adored.

    Ah ! how unjust to nature and himself,
Is thoughtless, thankless, inconsistent man !
Like children babbling nonsense in their sports,
* We censure nature for a span too short ;
That span too short, we tax as tedious too ;
Torture invention, all expedients tire,
To lash the ling'ring moments into speed,
And whirl us, happy riddance ! from ourselves.
Art, brainless art ! our furious charioteer,
For nature's voice unstifled would recall,
Drives headlong tow'rds the precipice of death—
Death, most our dread ; death thus more dreadful made
O what a riddle of absurdity !
Leisure is pain ; take off our chariot-wheels,
How heavily we drag the load of life !
Blest leisure is our curse ; like that of Cain,
It makes us wander ; wander earth around
To fly that tyrant, thought. As Atlas groan'd
The world beneath, we groan beneath an hour :
We cry for mercy to the next amusement ;
The next amusement mortgages our fields—
Slight inconvenience ! prisons hardly frown—
From hateful time if prisons set us free ;
Yet when death kindly tenders us relief,
We call him cruel ; years to moments shrink,
Ages to years : the telescope is turn'd,

PL. 9. ENGRAVING FOR YOUNG'S NIGHTS.
GRAVURE POUR LES NUITS DE YOUNG.
STICH FÜR YOUNGS « NÄCHTE ».
INTAGLIO PER LE NOTTI DI YOUNG.
GRABADO PARA LAS NOCHES DE YOUNG.

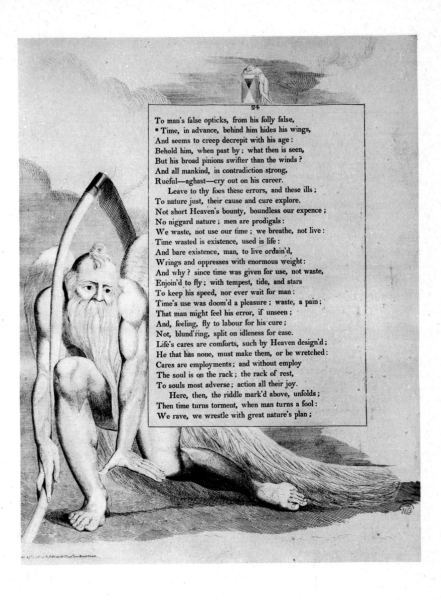

24

To man's false opticks, from his folly false,
* Time, in advance, behind him hides his wings,
And seems to creep decrepit with his age:
Behold him, when past by; what then is seen,
But his broad pinions swifter than the winds?
And all mankind, in contradiction strong,
Rueful—aghast—cry out on his career.

Leave to thy foes these errors, and these ills;
To nature just, their cause and cure explore.
Not short Heaven's bounty, boundless our expence;
No niggard nature; men are prodigals:
We waste, not use our time; we breathe, not live:
Time wasted is existence, used is life:
And bare existence, man, to live ordain'd,
Wrings and oppresses with enormous weight:
And why? since time was given for use, not waste,
Enjoin'd to fly; with tempest, tide, and stars
To keep his speed, nor ever wait for man:
Time's use was doom'd a pleasure; waste, a pain;
That man might feel his error, if unseen;
And, feeling, fly to labour for his cure;
Not, blund'ring, split on idleness for ease.
Life's cares are comforts, such by Heaven design'd;
He that has none, must make them, or be wretched:
Cares are employments; and without employ
The soul is on the rack; the rack of rest,
To souls most adverse; action all their joy.

Here, then, the riddle mark'd above, unfolds;
Then time turns torment, when man turns a fool:
We rave, we wrestle with great nature's plan;

PL. 10. ENGRAVING FOR YOUNG'S NIGHTS.
GRAVURE POUR LES NUITS DE YOUNG.
STICH FÜR YOUNGS « NÄCHTE ».
INTAGLIO PER LE NOTTI DI YOUNG.
GRABADO PARA LAS NOCHES DE YOUNG.

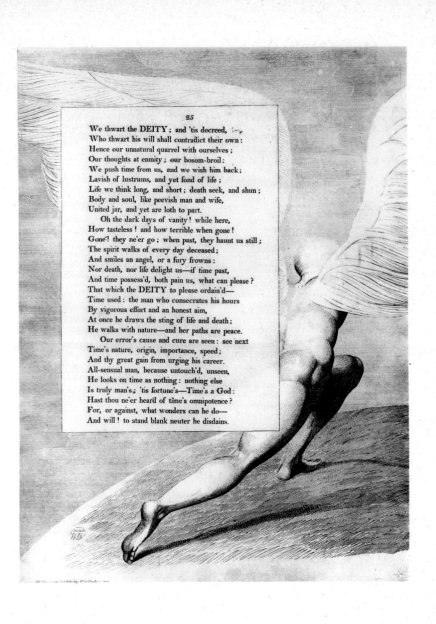

We thwart the DEITY; and 'tis decreed,
Who thwart his will shall contradict their own:
Hence our unnatural quarrel with ourselves;
Our thoughts at enmity; our bosom-broil:
We push time from us, and we wish him back;
Lavish of lustrums, and yet fond of life;
Life we think long, and short; death seek, and shun;
Body and soul, like peevish man and wife,
United jar, and yet are loth to part.

    Oh the dark days of vanity! while here,
How tasteless! and how terrible when gone!
Gone! they ne'er go; when past, they haunt us still;
The spirit walks of every day deceased;
And smiles an angel, or a fury frowns:
Nor death, nor life delight us—if time past,
And time possess'd, both pain us, what can please?
That which the DEITY to please ordain'd—
Time used: the man who consecrates his hours
By vigorous effort and an honest aim,
At once he draws the sting of life and death;
He walks with nature—and her paths are peace.

    Our error's cause and cure are seen: see next
Time's nature, origin, importance, speed;
And thy great gain from urging his career.
All-sensual man, because untouch'd, unseen,
He looks on time as nothing: nothing else
Is truly man's; 'tis fortune's—Time's a God:
Hast thou ne'er heard of time's omnipotence?
For, or against, what wonders can he do—
And will! to stand blank neuter he disdains.

PL. II. ENGRAVING FOR YOUNG'S NIGHTS.
GRAVURE POUR LES NUITS DE YOUNG.
STICH FÜR YOUNGS « NÄCHTE ».
INTAGLIO PER LE NOTTI DI YOUNG.
GRABADO PARA LAS NOCHES DE YOUNG.

And then, where are we? where, LORENZO, then
Thy sports—thy pomps?—I grant thee, in a state
Not unambitious; in the ruffled shroud,
Thy parian tomb's triumphant arch beneath:
Has death his fopperies? then well may life
Put on her plume, and in her rainbow shine.
    Ye well-array'd! ye lilies of our land!
Ye lilies male! who neither toil, nor spin,
As sister lilies might;—if not so wise
As Solomon, more sumptuous to the sight!
Ye delicate! who nothing can support,
Yourselves most insupportable! for whom
The winter rose must blow, the sun put on
A brighter beam in Leo, silky-soft
Favonius breathe still softer, or be chid;
And other worlds send odours, sauce, and song,
And robes, and notions framed in foreign looms!
O ye LORENZOS of our age! who deem
One moment unamused, a misery
Not made for feeble man; who call aloud
For every bauble, drivell'd o'er by sense,
For rattles and conceits of every cast,
For change of follies and relays of joy,
To drag your patience through the tedious length
Of a short winter's day—say—sages; say
Wit's oracles; say—dreamers of gay dreams;
How will you weather an eternal night,
Where such expedients fail?
    * O treacherous conscience! while she seems to sleep
On rose and myrtle, lull'd with syren song;

NIGHT

THE

THIRD,

NARCISSA.

PL. 13. ENGRAVING FOR YOUNG'S NIGHTS.
GRAVURE POUR LES NUITS DE YOUNG.
STICH FÜR YOUNGS « NÄCHTE ».
INTAGLIO PER LE NOTTI DI YOUNG.
GRABADO PARA LAS NOCHES DE YOUNG.

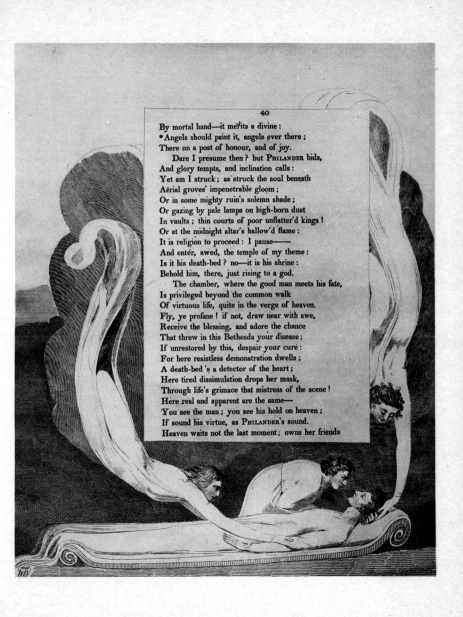

40

By mortal hand—it merits a divine :
*Angels should paint it, angels ever there ;
There on a post of honour, and of joy.

    Dare I presume then ? but PHILANDER bids,
And glory tempts, and inclination calls :
Yet am I struck ; as struck the soul beneath
Aërial groves' impenetrable gloom ;
Or in some mighty ruin's solemn shade ;
Or gazing by pale lamps on high-born dust
In vaults ; thin courts of poor unflatter'd kings !
Or at the midnight altar's hallow'd flame :
It is religion to proceed : I pause——
And entér, awed, the temple of my theme :
Is it his death-bed ? no—it is his shrine :
Behold him, there, just rising to a god.

    The chamber, where the good man meets his fate,
Is privileged beyond the common walk
Of virtuous life, quite in the verge of heaven.
Fly, ye profane ! if not, draw near with awe,
Receive the blessing, and adore the chance
That threw in this Bethesda your disease ;
If unrestored by this, despair your cure :
For here resistless demonstration dwells ;
A death-bed 's a detector of the heart ;
Here tired dissimulation drops her mask,
Through life's grimace that mistress of the scene !
Here real and apparent are the same—
You see the man ; you see his hold on heaven ;
If sound his virtue, as PHILANDER's sound.
Heaven waits not the last moment ; owns her friends

PL. 14. ENGRAVING FOR YOUNG'S NIGHTS.
GRAVURE POUR LES NUITS DE YOUNG.
STICH FÜR YOUNGS « NÄCHTE ».
INTAGLIO PER LE NOTTI DI YOUNG.
GRABADO PARA LAS NOCHES DE YOUNG.

41

On this side death; and points them out to men:
A lecture silent, but of sovereign power!
To vice, confusion; and to virtue, peace.

    Whatever farce the boastful hero plays,
Virtue alone has majesty in death;
And greater still, the more the tyrant frowns:
PHILANDER! he severely frown'd on thee:
" No warning given—unceremonious fate!
" A sudden rush from life's meridian joys!
" A wrench from all we love—from all we are!
" A restless bed of pain! a plunge opaque
" Beyond conjecture! feeble nature's dread!
" Strong reason's shudder at the dark unknown!
" A sun extinguish'd! a just opening grave!
" And oh! the last—last—what? can words express?
" Thought reach? the last, last—silence of a friend!"
Where are those horrors, that amazement where,
This hideous group of ills, which singly shock?
Demand from man—I thought him man till now.

    Through nature's wreck, through vanquish'd agonies,
Like the stars struggling through this midnight gloom,
What gleams of joy! what more than human peace!
Where, the frail mortal? the poor abject worm?
No, not in death, the mortal to be found.
His conduct is a legacy for all,
Richer than Mammon's for his single heir:
His comforters he comforts; great in ruin,
With unreluctant grandeur gives, not yields
His soul sublime; and closes with his fate.

PL. 15. ENGRAVING FOR YOUNG'S NIGHTS.
GRAVURE POUR LES NUITS DE YOUNG.
STICH FÜR YOUNGS « NÄCHTE ».
INTAGLIO PER LE NOTTI DI YOUNG.
GRABADO PARA LAS NOCHES DE YOUNG.

46

Or if we wish a fourth, it is a friend——
But friends how mortal! dangerous the desire.
　　Take Phœbus to yourselves, ye basking bards!
Inebriate at fair fortune's fountain-head;
And reeling through the wilderness of joy;
* Where sense runs savage broke from reason's chain,
And sings false peace, till smother'd by the pall.
My fortune is unlike; unlike my song;
Unlike the DEITY my song invokes.
I to day's soft-eyed sister pay my court,
Endymion's rival! and her aid implore;
Now first implored in succour to the muse.
　　Thou who didst lately borrow Cynthia's form,
And modestly forego thine own! O thou
Who didst thyself, at midnight hours, inspire!
Say, why not Cynthia patroness of song?
As thou her crescent, she thy character
Assumes; still more a goddess by the change.
　　Are there demurring wits, who dare dispute
This revolution in the world inspired?
Ye train pierian! to the lunar sphere,
In silent hour address your ardent call
For aid immortal—less her brother's right.
She, with the spheres harmonious, nightly leads
The mazy dance, and hears their matchless strain;
A strain for gods, denied to mortal ear.
Transmit it heard, thou silver queen of heaven!
What title or what name endears thee most?
Cynthia! Cyllene! Phœbe!—or dost hear
With higher gust fair P——d of the skies?

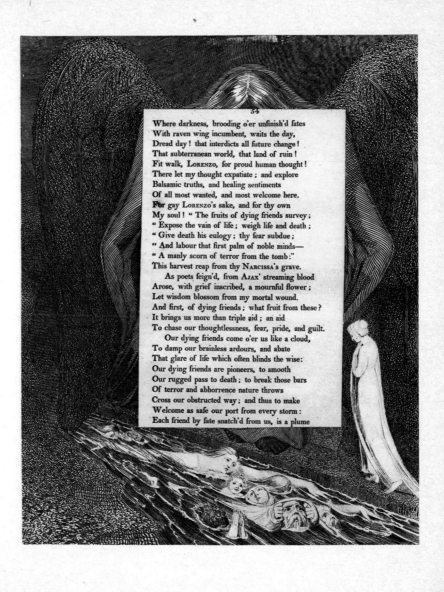

54

Where darkness, brooding o'er unfinish'd fates
With raven wing incumbent, waits the day,
Dread day! that interdicts all future change!
That subterranean world, that land of ruin!
Fit walk, LORENZO, for proud human thought!
There let my thought expatiate; and explore
Balsamic truths, and healing sentiments
Of all most wanted, and most welcome here.
For gay LORENZO's sake, and for thy own
My soul! "The fruits of dying friends survey;
" Expose the vain of life; weigh life and death;
" Give death his eulogy; thy fear subdue;
" And labour that first palm of noble minds—
" A manly scorn of terror from the tomb:"
This harvest reap from thy NARCISSA's grave.

    As poets feign'd, from AJAX' streaming blood
Arose, with grief inscribed, a mournful flower;
Let wisdom blossom from my mortal wound.
And first, of dying friends; what fruit from these?
It brings us more than triple aid; an aid
To chase our thoughtlessness, fear, pride, and guilt.

    Our dying friends come o'er us like a cloud,
To damp our brainless ardours, and abate
That glare of life which often blinds the wise:
Our dying friends are pioneers, to smooth
Our rugged pass to death; to break those bars
Of terror and abhorrence nature throws
Cross our obstructed way; and thus to make
Welcome as safe our port from every storm:
Each friend by fate snatch'd from us, is a plume

To dust when drop proud nature's proudest spheres,
And live entire: death is the crown of life;
Were death denied, poor man would live in vain;
Were death denied, to live would not be life;
Were death denied, even fools would wish to die:
Death wounds to cure: we fall, we rise, we reign!
Spring from our fetters, fasten in the skies
Where blooming Eden withers in our sight.
Death gives us more than was in Eden lost;
*This KING OF TERRORS is the PRINCE OF PEACE.
When shall I die to vanity, pain, death?
When shall I die?—when shall I live for ever?

PL. 19. NAOMI AND RUTH.
NOÉMI ET RUTH.
NAEMI UND RUTH.
NOEMI E RUT.
NOEMI Y RUTH.

PL. 20. DAVID DELIVERED OUT OF MANY WATERS.
DAVID SAUVÉ DES EAUX.
DAVID AUS DEN WASSERN ERRETTET.
DAVIDE SALVATO DELLE AQUE.
DAVID SALVADO DE LAS AGUAS.

PL. 21. THE PROCESSION FROM CALVARY.
LA PROCESSION APRÈS LE CALVAIRE.
PROZESSION NACH DEN LEIDENSSTATIONEN.
LA PROCESSIONE DOPO IL CALVARIO.
LA PROCESION DESPUÉS DEL CALVARIO.

PL. 23. DRAWING FOR THE GRAVE OF BLAIR.
DESSIN POUR LE TOMBEAU DE BLAIR.
ZEICHNUNG FÜR DAS GRABMAL BLAIR'S.
DISEGNO PER IL SEPOLCRO DEL BLAIR.
DIBUJO PARA EL SEPULCRO DE BLAIR.

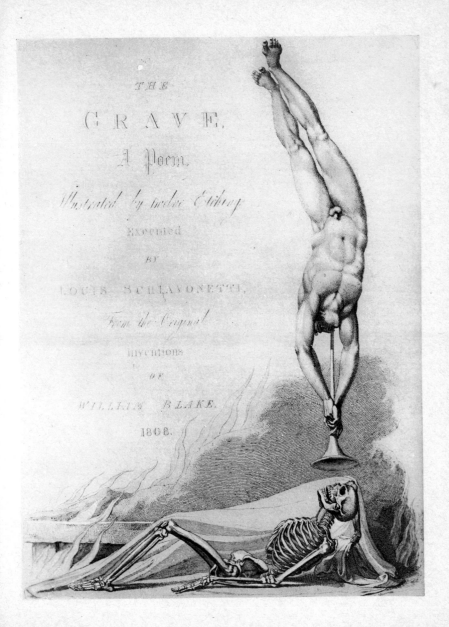

THE

GRAVE,

A Poem

Illustrated by twelve Etchings

Executed

BY

LOUIS SCHIAVONETTI,

From the Original

Inventions

OF

WILLIAM BLAKE.

1808.

Drawn by W. Blake.　　　　　　　　*Etched by L. Schiavonetti.*

The meeting of a Family in Heaven.

PL. 25. THE SOUL EXPLORING THE RECESSES OF THE GRAVE (THE GRAVE
OF BLAIR).

L'AME EXPLORANT LES REPLIS DE LA TOMBE (TOMBEAU DE
BLAIR).

ZWISCHEN DEN STEINERNEN FALTEN DES GRABES, DIE FOR-
SCHENDE SEELE (DAS GRABMAL BLAIR'S).

L'ANIMA ESAMINANTE LE PIEGHE DEL SEPOLCRO (IL SEPOLCRO
DEL BLAIR).

LA ALMA EXPLORANDO LAS VUELTAS DEL SEPULCRO (EL SEPULCRO
DE BLAIR).

Designed by Wm. Blake.   Etched by L. Schiavonetti.

The Soul exploring the recesses of the Grave

PL. 26. DEATH'S DOOR (THE GRAVE OF BLAIR).
LA PORTE DE LA MORT (TOMBEAU DE BLAIR).
DAS TOR DES TODES (DAS GRABMAL BLAIR'S).
LA PORTA DELLA MORTE (IL SEPOLCRO DEL BLAIR).
LA PUERTA DE LA MUERTE (EL SEPULCRO DE BLAIR).

Drawn by W. Blake.   Etched by L. Schiavonetti.

Christ descending into the Grave.

Eternal King! whose potent Arm sustains
The Keys of Hell and Death.

London, Published May 1.1808, by R. Ackermann 101 Strand.

PL. 28. THE DEATH OF THE GOOD OLD MAN (THE GRAVE OF BLAIR).
MORT DU BON VIEILLARD (TOMBEAU DE BLAIR).
TOD DES WACKEREN GREISES (DAS GRABMAL BLAIR'S).
LA MORTE DEL BUONO VECCHIO (IL SEPOLCRO DEL BLAIR).
LA MUERTE DEL BUEN VIEJO (EL SEPULCRO DE BLAIR).

The Death of S.t [?] Jos.pub.d [?] 181[?]

PL. 29. THE SOUL HOVERING OVER THE BODY RELUCTANTLY PARTING
  WITH LIFE (THE GRAVE OF BLAIR).

L'AME PLANANT AU-DESSUS DU CORPS SE SÉPARE AVEC REGRET
  DE LA VIE (TOMBEAU DE BLAIR).

DIE SEELE SCHWEBT ÜBER DEM KÖRPER UND TRENNT SICH
  UNGERN VOM LEBEN (DAS GRABMAL BLAIR'S).

L'ANIMA VOLANTE SOPRA IL CORPO LASCIA CON RAMMARICO LA
  VITA (IL SEPOLCRO DEL BLAIR).

EL ALMA PLANEANDO SOBRE EL CUERPO SE SEPARA CON SENTI-
  MIENTO DE LA VIDA (EL SEPULCRO DE BLAIR).

Etched by L. Schiavonetti.

Inv.d by W. Blake.

The Soul hovering over the Body reluctantly parting with Life.

—————————— How wishfully she looks
On all she's leaving, now no longer her's!

London, Published May 1 1808 by R. Ackermann 101 Strand.

Drawn by W.Blake.   Etched by L. Schiavonetti.

The Day of Judgment.

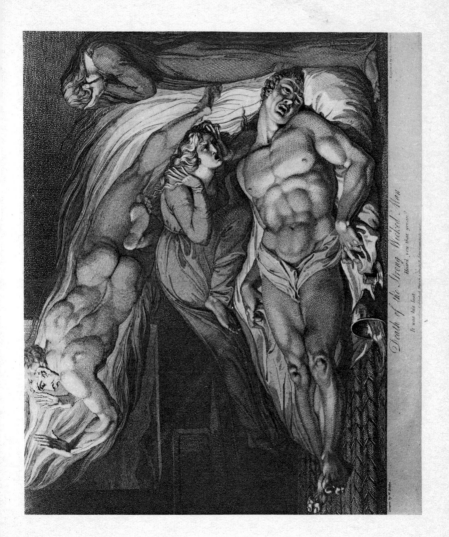

Death of the Strong Wicked Man

It was his last — Mortd, can thou give?

PL. 32. THE COUNSELLOR, KING, WARRIOR, MOTHER, AND CHILD IN THE TOMB (THE GRAVE OF BLAIR).

LE CONSEILLER, LE ROI, LE GUERRIER, LA MÈRE ET L'ENFANT DANS LA TOMBE (TOMBEAU DE BLAIR).

RAT, KÖNIG, KRIEGER, MUTTER UND KIND IM GRABE (DAS GRABMAL BLAIR'S).

IL CONSIGLIERE, IL RE, IL GUERRIERO, LA MADRE E IL FANCIULLO NELLA TOMBA (IL SEPOLCRO DEL BLAIR).

EL CONSEJERO, EL REY, EL GUERRERO, LA MADRE Y EL HIJO DENTRO DE LA TUMBA (EL SEPULCRO DE BLAIR).

Drawn by W. Blake.

London, Published 1 May 1808, by R. H. Ackermann 101 Strand.

The Counsellor, King, Warrior, Mother & Child, in the tomb.

PL. 33. THE DESCENT OF MAN INTO THE VALE OF DEATH (THE GRAVE
OF BLAIR).

LA DESCENTE DE L'HOMME DANS LA VALLÉE DE LA MORT (TOM-
BEAU DE BLAIR).

MENSCH DAS TODESTAL BETRETEND (DAS GRABMAL BLAIR'S).

LA DISCESA DELL'UOMO NELLA VALLATA DELLA MORTE (IL SE-
POLCRO DEL BLAIR).

EL HOMBRE BAJANDO AL VALLE DE LA MUERTE (EL SEPULCRO
DE BLAIR).

Engraved by L. Schiavonetti

The descent of Man into the Vale of Death.

'Tis here all meet'

London Published Mar 1 1813 by R. Ackermann, 101 Strand.

PL. 34. THE REUNION, OF THE SOUL AND THE BODY (THE GRAVE OF
BLAIR).
LA RÉUNION DE L'AME ET DU CORPS (TOMBEAU DE BLAIR).
VEREINIGUNG VON SEELE UND KÖRPER (DAS GRABMAL BLAIR'S).
LA RIUNIONE DELL'ANIMA E DEL CORPO (IL SEPOLCRO DEL BLAIR).
LA REUNION DEL ALMA Y DEL CUERPO (EL SEPULCRO DE BLAIR).

Drawn by W. Blake.   Published by L. Schiavonetti.

The Reunion of the Soul & the Body

PL. 35. THE HEALING OF THE WOMAN.
LA GUÉRISON DE LA FEMME.
HEILUNG DES WEIBES.
LA GUARIGIONE DELLA DONNA.
LA CURA DE LA MUJER.

PL. 36. WOMAN TAKEN IN ADULTARY.
LA FEMME ADULTÈRE.
DIE EHEBRECHERIN.
LA DONNA ADULTERA.
LA MUJER ADULTERÅ.

PL. 37. HARVEY'S MEDITATION.
LA MÉDITATION DE HARVEY.
HARVEY IM NACHSINNEN.
LA MEDITAZIONE DI HARVEY.
LA MEDITACION DE HARVEY.

PL. 39. SATAN WATCHING THE ENDEARMENT OF ADAM AND EVE.
SATAN ÉPIANT LES CARESSES D'ADAM ET D'ÈVE.
SATAN BELAUERT ADAM'S UND EVA'S LIEBKOSUNGEN.
SATANA CODIANTE LE CAREZZE DI ADAMO ED EVA.
SATANAS ESPIANDO LAS CARICIAS DE ADAN Y EVA.

PL. 40. THE CREATION OF EVE.
LA CRÉATION D'ÈVE.
EVA'S ERSCHAFFUNG.
LA CREAZIONE D'EVA.
LA CREACION DE EVA.